# Mindfulness Training in Sport

Darko Jekauc · Lea Mülberger · Susanne Weyland

# Mindfulness Training in Sport

An Exercise Program for Enhancing Athletic Performance

Darko Jekauc
Health Education and Sports Psychology
Karlsruhe Institute of Technology
Karlsruhe, Germany

Lea Mülberger
Karlsruhe, Germany

Susanne Weyland
Karlsruhe Institute of Technology
Karlsruhe, Germany

ISBN 978-3-662-68803-8 ISBN 978-3-662-68804-5 (eBook)
https://doi.org/10.1007/978-3-662-68804-5

Translation from the German language edition: "Achtsamkeitstraining im Sport" by Darko Jekauc et al.,
© Der/die Herausgeber bzw. der/die Autor(en), exklusiv lizenziert an Springer-Verlag GmbH, DE, ein Teil
von Springer Nature 2022. Published by Springer Berlin Heidelberg. All Rights Reserved.

This book is a translation of the original German edition "Achtsamkeitstraining im Sport" by Darko Jekauc,
Lea Mülberger and Susanne Weyland published by Springer-Verlag GmbH, DE in 2022. The translation was
done with the help of an artificial intelligence machine translation tool. A subsequent human revision was
done primarily in terms of content, so that the book will read stylistically differently from a conventional
translation. Springer Nature works continuously to further the development of tools for the production of
books and on the related technologies to support the authors.

© The Editor(s) (if applicable) and The Author(s), under exclusive license to Springer-Verlag GmbH, DE,
part of Springer Nature 2024

This work is subject to copyright. All rights are solely and exclusively licensed by the Publisher, whether
the whole or part of the material is concerned, specifically the rights of translation, reprinting, reuse
of illustrations, recitation, broadcasting, reproduction on microfilms or in any other physical way, and
transmission or information storage and retrieval, electronic adaptation, computer software, or by similar or
dissimilar methodology now known or hereafter developed.
The use of general descriptive names, registered names, trademarks, service marks, etc. in this publication does
not imply, even in the absence of a specific statement, that such names are exempt from the relevant protective
laws and regulations and therefore free for general use.
The publisher, the authors, and the editors are safe to assume that the advice and information in this book
are believed to be true and accurate at the date of publication. Neither the publisher nor the authors or the
editors give a warranty, expressed or implied, with respect to the material contained herein or for any errors
or omissions that may have been made. The publisher remains neutral with regard to jurisdictional claims in
published maps and institutional affiliations.

This Springer imprint is published by the registered company Springer-Verlag GmbH, DE, part of Springer
Nature.
The registered company address is: Heidelberger Platz 3, 14197 Berlin, Germany

Paper in this product is recyclable.

# Preface

As an aspiring tennis player, I aimed for top performance and did everything to achieve success. I invested time and energy and tried to push myself and my body to peak performance. However, at some point, I noticed that I was very tense and increasingly getting in my own way. Especially in important competitions and matches, I played far below my performance limit, occasionally plunging into crises that affected not only my performance but also led to emotional lows. I could hardly explain the large performance fluctuations. The curiosity to understand what was going on in my head drove me to read a multitude of sports psychology books, complete a degree in psychology, write a doctoral thesis in sports psychology, and attend some further education courses in the field of applied sports psychology.

I realized that I was not the only one confronted with this problem of performance fluctuation and that competition anxiety, lack of serenity, loss of self-confidence, and concentration are the central issues of sports psychology. As part of these training and further education courses, I got to know a number of sports psychology tools and I willingly tried them out on myself or in collaboration with other athletes. However, I noticed that these classic tools of sports psychology only treated the symptoms of these problems and did not tackle the problem at its root.

Quite by chance, while reading the contributions to the latest findings in brain research, I learned that certain mindfulness practices, which I had not known at all until then, produce noticeable changes in the brain. The mindfulness practices target the brain centers responsible for the perception of one's own feelings and thoughts, emotion regulation, concentration, and serenity. I immediately understood the potential that mindfulness practices have to address the problems of sports psychology. My research revealed that, although mindfulness was hardly known in sports psychology, it had already found resonance in the practice of elite sports. Some high-performance athletes practiced mindfulness intuitively to optimize their performance at a psychological level.

Therefore, I immediately signed up for mindfulness courses, visited meditation centers, and practiced these techniques myself. I noticed that most of the courses were of a spiritual nature, tinged with religious ideas, and were of little use for application in sports practice. Therefore, I began to extract relevant mindfulness practices that seemed promising for sports practice and have a scientific foundation. In collaboration with some scientists, practitioners (especially with Christoph Kittler), and numerous athletes, I experimented until a concrete program was developed in the sports psychology context. The program was tested in several studies and continuously adapted to the needs of the athletes. The product of this years-long work is the present book.

This book is aimed at practitioners in sports, such as athletes, coaches, sports psychologists, and all those interested in applied sports psychology. It offers a practice-oriented introduction to the topic of mindfulness in sports and a tried-and-tested program. This book consists of two sections: I) Theoretical and empirical foundations and II) The Program.

In the first section of the book, the foundations of sports psychology are laid in two chapters. The first chapter elaborates on the importance of emotions for competitive sports. We can be drawn into the vortex of the cycle of emotions, which can plunge us into crises. Ways are shown on how to break the cycle of emotions and achieve more emotional stability. The second chapter presents the history of mindfulness in sports and how mindfulness has found its way from an Eastern tradition into the NBA, Grand Slams, and World Championships. Stories are told about athletes and coaches who have successfully transferred the training of mindfulness into competitive sports.

The second section of the book deals with the mindfulness program and the third chapter of the book outlines the principles of mindfulness training, the development, and the structure of the program. The course consists of eight course units, each unit representing another chapter (Chap. 4–11). In these eight chapters, guidance is given on how the course can be implemented in practice. In addition to the descriptions of the exercises and the course sequence, course materials are also included in this book.

You are now embarking on an exciting journey that will certainly provide new impulses for your own sports practice. Processes will be stimulated that favor a transformation in which more acceptance, serenity, and emotional stability should emerge. It will be a long journey where not everything will work out immediately, but it is definitely worth a try.

Enjoy reading the book and practicing mindfulness!

March 31, 2022                                                                 Darko Jekauc

# Contents

**Part I   Theoretical and Empirical Foundations**

**1   Importance of Emotions in Sports**                                        3
   1.1   From an Opportunity to a Trauma                          3
   1.2   From the Hunted to the Hunter                            6
   1.3   The Cycle of Emotions                                    8
   1.4   Way Out of the Cycle                                     13
   References                                                     16

**2   History of Mindfulness in Sports**                                        17
   2.1   Far Eastern Traditions                                   17
   2.2   The Bible of Sports Psychology                           18
   2.3   Mindfulness Finds Its Way into the NBA                   21
   2.4   The Legacy of Phil Jackson                               23
   2.5   A Man with Nerves of Steel                               27
   2.6   A Leap to Greater Inner Strength                         30
   2.7   Effects of Mindfulness Training in Competitive
       and Elite Sports                       32
   References                                                     34

**Part II   The Program**

**3   The Mindfulness Program for Athletes**                                    39
   3.1   Principles of Mindfulness Training in Sports             39
   3.2   What is Mindfulness and How Does it Work?                42
   3.3   Development of the Program                               44

**x    Contents**

| | | |
|---|---|---|
| | 3.4    Efficacy Verification | 46 |
| | 3.5    Course Structure | 47 |
| | References | 50 |
| **4** | **Course Unit 1: Mindfulness—Arriving in the Here and Now** | **53** |
| | References | 64 |
| **5** | **Course Unit 2: Mindfulness as a Means of Self-Realization** | **65** |
| **6** | **Course Unit 3: Deepening the Topic of Breath Meditation** | **75** |
| | References | 82 |
| **7** | **Course Unit 4: Body Perception—The Key to Emotions** | **83** |
| | References | 91 |
| **8** | **Course Unit 5: Perception of Thoughts** | **93** |
| | References | 100 |
| **9** | **Course Unit 6: Perception of Feelings** | **101** |
| | Reference | 107 |
| **10** | **Course Unit 7: Promoting Positive Feelings** | **109** |
| | References | 115 |
| **11** | **Course Unit 8: Building Mindfulness** | **117** |
| | References | 123 |

# Part I

# Theoretical and Empirical Foundations

# 1

# Importance of Emotions in Sports

## 1.1 From an Opportunity to a Trauma

In the tennis hall of a provincial club in Württemberg, I (Darko Jekauc) experienced a personal drama that would mentally burden me for years and significantly influence my behavior on the court. The initial situation was promising. After I, as a youth player, had easily beaten a rather weak opponent in the first round of this men's indoor tournament, I faced Michael in the second round. I believed I could beat him, even though he was seeded. I had known him for two years, as he had trained with us in the club several times. Michael was a small and agile player, one who let his opponent take the lead, only to counter from impossible positions with spectacular shots. Although he had a much higher ranking than me and played two leagues above me, I thought I had a good chance of winning this match too. I was in good shape and had nothing to lose as the supposedly weaker opponent. If I were to lose, everyone would say that my opponent had been much more experienced and ranked much higher. If I were to win, however, it would be a great success for me.

With this attitude, I went into the match. My muscles felt loose, even though I was hitting the balls hard. Michael rarely managed to return my serves in a controlled manner. I dominated the match from the start, forcing him to make mistakes. Consequently, I won the first set and secured a comfortable lead with a break advantage in the second set. It was surprising how calmly Michael played, even though he was trailing against a young and significantly lower-ranked player. Tirelessly, he ran from one corner to the

---

© The Author(s), under exclusive license to Springer-Verlag GmbH, DE, part of Springer Nature 2024
D. Jekauc et al., *Mindfulness Training in Sport*,
https://doi.org/10.1007/978-3-662-68804-5_1

other, trying to use his acrobatic shots as counters. But it seemed as if my balls were too fast for him that day. At a score of 5:3 in the second set, I had a match point on Michael's serve. I was already imagining how I, as one of the youngest participants in the tournament, would advance to the quarter-finals. I had trained hard for such a moment; I had earned this success.

Suddenly, however, my seemingly secure victory was in danger. At the first match point, I worked out the chance for a direct point win after a long rally. Victory was within reach. Full of determination and as hard as I could, I played the ball into Michael's backhand corner. But the felt ball landed a few centimeters behind the line. Michael called out "Out!" with relish. Disappointed, I briefly slumped, but immediately straightened up again. "Well, I'll just have to work out a second match point," I thought. Said and done. I used a similar tactic as at the first match point. I chased Michael from right to left several times and stormed—at what seemed to me a favorable moment—to the net. But Michael passed me, fended off the match point again, and shouted a loud "Come on!" through the hall. This scream hit me to the core. Suddenly, I felt a strong excitement. My hands started to sweat, my breath felt constricted. At that moment, I began to doubt whether I would win this match. I wondered what would happen if I were to lose after all. Although only a few points separated me from victory, I saw myself facing an almost insurmountable chasm that I had to overcome to win the match. The lead, which had given me security throughout the match, suddenly felt like a burden. How humiliating would it feel if I were to lose this match after all?

Deeply insecure, I played the next points. My shots suddenly felt weak and powerless. Michael sensed my insecurity and now played boldly and offensively. At a score of 5:4 for me, I had every reason to stay calm. Throughout the match, I had brought my service games through without major problems. But this time, my hands were so sweaty that I could hardly hold the racket, hardly serve. Several double faults were followed by very soft serves, which Michael sometimes directly converted into points. So this game went smoothly to him.

To my surprise, the loss of the game to 5:5 brought a certain relief. The match was now open again. I no longer felt the pressure to have to win the next game. We both brought our service games through, and so it went into the tiebreak. I got off to a better start and earned two mini-breaks. At a score of 6:3 for me, I had three match points, even two on my own serve. At this moment, the oppressive feeling of insecurity rose in me again. My hands were sweaty again, my feet felt blocked. I played a very soft serve into the field and hoped that Michael would make a mistake. He sensed my

# 1 Importance of Emotions in Sports 5

insecurity again and chased me across the entire court until he finally made the point. Now I had also squandered this match point.

For my next match point, I thought: "You can lose, but not like this! Take a risk!" I placed a soft, but heavily cut serve on Michael's backhand and moved to the net. Michael hadn't expected this variation, and he returned a soft and half-high backhand slice ball through the middle. Now I had the huge chance to make the point with a well-placed volley. But I ran hesitantly to the ball, as if I had to drag a 100 kg load behind me. My volley ball was well placed on my opponent's side, but it was much too slow and much too high. Michael moved forward decisively and passed me. Again, a loud "Come on" from him followed. I was full of despair, lamenting how one could play a volley so poorly, bemoaning my inability.

It happened as it had to. Those who do not take their chances are punished hard. I lost the tiebreak 6:8. In the third set, I kept thinking about how I could have squandered my chances. My emotions had completely taken hold of me. On the one hand, I acted very fearfully and inhibited, on the other, I was very angry. I reacted irritably to the smallest mistakes, and my game fluctuated between paralyzing defensiveness and reckless offensiveness. Either I just pushed the balls into the field or I hammered them with incalculable risk. Michael benefited from my struggle with myself, easily decided the third set 6:1, and thus won the match.

My disappointment after the match was huge. I had been on the verge of victory against such a good player, had dominated the match in terms of gameplay. The manner of the defeat occupied me for quite a while. I was still blaming myself several days after the match, wondering how I could have let the match slip out of my hands so close to the goal.

After two weeks, it seemed as if the defeat no longer bothered me as much. I signed up for the next tournament. There, I had to realize that I had not yet processed my failure. At first, everything went well—until the match point. Then the old fears came back. My hands started to sweat, my feet felt paralyzed again. In order to convert the match point, my opponent had to make a mistake. Even against weak opponents, I found it hard to win. Against equal opponents, my fear had a devastating effect. It now always crept up on me at other important points like break balls or set balls. The problem seemed to be getting bigger and bigger.

I talked to my coach and some of my friends about it and received different advice. Some said I just needed to keep using fresh grip tapes so I could hold the racket even when I was sweating. Others said I should "believe in myself", "just stay relaxed", "focus only on the next point" or "think positively". I was annoyed by such general advice. Someone who has never played competitive sports thinks it's easy. Probably these very people would have panicked or lost interest and given up if they had been in a similar situation to me. If only they knew how helpless it feels when you lose all control over your own fears and physical states. It seemed as if no one had a solution to my problem. To save myself anger and frustration, I decided not to talk about this problem anymore and not to play tournaments for a while.

It is an irony of fate that a chance has turned into a trauma. I had nothing to lose and yet this defeat has thrown me into the abyss of negative emotions. In this match, I beat myself. Michael had lured me into dangerous waters, but I had gotten myself into the whirlpool of negative emotions. Once you're in the vortex, it's hard to get out if you're not a trained swimmer. Only much later did I understand that behind serenity and emotional stability there is a lot of training. You have to invest something to strengthen the mental muscle.

Losing a match narrowly is not a disaster. Losing is a central part of competitive sports. If you want to reach the shore of success, you have to swim through the waters of defeat. But emotions have something absolute about them that does not allow for relativization. If someone had told me before the match that I would lose only very narrowly against such a good player, I would have been satisfied. In retrospect, I only saw the missed opportunity and not the good performance I had made to bring a strong player to the brink of defeat. Rationally, I could have seen the narrow defeat as a success. On the emotional side, the defeat felt terrible.

The fatal thing about the cycle of emotions is that it has a mammoth memory. When you get into a similar situation again, the original emotions hit you with full force. Past negative experiences suddenly come alive again. The trapdoor to the whirlpool of negative emotions suddenly opens again under your own feet and you fall in before you realize it.

## 1.2 From the Hunted to the Hunter

The summer season came and I had to face the challenge and my fear again. When I encountered weaker opponents, I somehow struggled my way to victory. With every match won, a huge weight was lifted from my heart, because I had not plunged into the abyss again. Against equal opponents, my handicap was a real problem. So I dragged my fear from match to match, from tournament to tournament. The self-confidence was no longer there. The fear of another fiasco felt worse than the defeats themselves.

# 1 Importance of Emotions in Sports 7

Over time, I developed my own strategies for dealing with my fear. I noticed that I could keep the fear at bay for a while by being aggressive. Anger and aggression are initially less aversive emotions than fear. You feel full of energy and drive, instead of tensing up. The feeling of helplessness was initially eliminated. I shouted on the court, pushed myself loudly, picked fights with opponents and convinced myself that I had to hate them to play well. There were some ugly scenes on the court, but this strategy seemed to help me. Whenever fear arose, I tried to turn it into aggression. My results gradually returned. I also started winning close matches again, turning lost games in my favor.

I intuitively felt that the aggression not only helped me keep the fear at bay, but also influenced the opponent. Some players felt insulted by my loud shouting, some intimidated, others were annoyed with me and yet others picked fights with me. Only a few remained cool and showed no reaction. I noticed that my aggressive behavior had different effects at different stages of the match. So I started to separate the aggression from my fear and use it as an independent means to an end.

I experimented with how intimidation affected certain opponents at certain stages of the match. With some opponents, it worked from the start, with others, it only worked as a surprise. But I also noticed that the aggression cost me a lot of energy and therefore had to be used judiciously. If I pushed myself too early and too much throughout the match, I had too little strength left at the end of the match. If I pushed myself too intensely, there was a risk that the situation would get out of control. In some cases, my aggression also turned against myself. Every match felt like a ride on the razor's edge. It was about finding the right measure. I watched my opponents closely, how they reacted to small provocations and developed a battle plan, when I should stay calm and when I should come out of hiding.

From being the hunted, I became a hunter, driving other players into the abyss of their emotions. The majority of my opponents hated me for it and avoided me even after the match. For me, aggression became a tactical measure to win the matches. I crossed a line of good behavior because I knew it would bother my opponents. I didn't care what others thought of me at the time. The goal was to give everything to win the matches. I thought to myself: The fight takes place on the court and after the match, we can get along again, no matter how it turned out.

Many took my intimidations as an attack on their person and wanted nothing to do with me. I earned the image of a bad boy. At tournaments, players nudged each other and said, "Watch out for this guy! He can throw you off balance". I also won some matches against significantly stronger opponents because they fell into my trap. I decided some games from a hopeless situation for me, which earned me the reputation of a psycho warrior among my friends from the club. Some admired me, some hated me, but no one liked to play against me. Who wants to play against a "psycho"?

Although this strategy had already brought me one or another spectacular victory, I intuitively knew that these successes were based only on the weaknesses of my opponents. There was still a lot of room for improvement in my own development. I just didn't know to what extent. But I had understood that I was far from emotional stability. Players like Pete Sampras, who once dominated the tennis scene, were anything but emotional or even aggressive. At that time, I could not imagine that calmness, concentration and emotional stability are the product of hard work. They require the athlete to fundamentally change his attitude towards life.

Some observers asked me how I manage to unsettle my opponents so much and bring about radical turns in the match. My answer was always that it's my secret. In fact, I was not clear about what was happening on the court. I only knew that my aggressive behavior affects me and my opponent at certain stages of the match. Why this is so and what processes are behind it, I was not aware. Only much later, after studying psychology and writing a doctoral thesis in sports psychology, did I begin to understand that emotional processes were at work. These processes influence our performance in sports much more strongly than was assumed until recently.

## 1.3 The Cycle of Emotions

Anyone who has ever played competitive sports knows that it can get emotional in the fight for victory and defeat. Emotions can help us surpass ourselves and call up our best performances. But they can also plunge us into a deep crisis. These highs and lows sometimes last only a few moments, but they can also last for days, weeks or even months. We often observe marked turns in matches, where a player or a team dominates the match with great dominance and then suddenly, for hardly comprehensible reasons, it tips in favor of the opponent. In my match against Michael, the match points were certainly the turning point of the match, both in terms of the outcome of the match and emotionally. The feeling of confidence and dominance had given way to a state of fear and despair; I had fallen into the cycle of negative emotions.

The cycle of emotions (Jekauc et al., 2021) always follows a certain pattern. It can be represented as a system that operates according to the principles of positive feedback. A starting value, e.g., an emotional reaction after losing a point, triggers a chain reaction that continually reactivates itself and further amplifies the starting value. For example, a performance that led to a loss of a point is influenced by emotional factors in such a way that the probability of losing the point increases in the next ball exchange. If the emotional chain reaction is triggered several times in a row, the course of a game can take a completely new turn. A player who was superior in the first set becomes the inferior player after a series of point losses. The balance of power between the two opponents in this match has shifted. Small changes have large and hardly predictable effects. Responsible for this radical change is the emotional cycle, which consists of six components: a trigger, physical reactions, action tendencies, emotional expression, feeling, and cognitions (Fig. 1.1).

*Trigger.* The trigger is the spark plug in the engine of emotions. The triggering process represents an automated mechanism that sets off a chain reaction. It is an unconscious process that cannot be controlled voluntarily, but can still be altered through learning processes. A common trigger for an emotional reaction in competitive sports is the pressure that arises from the interplay of two factors: *expectations* and *consequences.* If the consequences of the match for us or our self-esteem are very high and the expectations of the

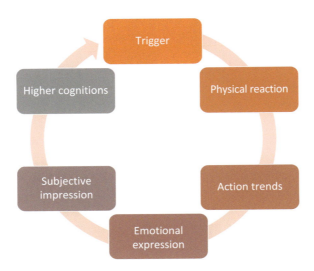

**Fig. 1.1** The cycle of emotions

course of the match are not met, the cycle of emotions is set in motion. Fear is particularly triggered in this way.

*Expectations* represent target values against which we evaluate situations. They act like a bar in high jump. If it is knocked down, this marks a negative event. If the target values are met, e.g., by leading against a weaker opponent, then the situation and one's own performance are assessed positively or at least neutrally. Failure to meet expectations leads to a negative assessment of one's own situation, which can be considered the origin of a negative emotion. The emotional reaction will be stronger the greater the expectation before a competition. For example, if you compete against a supposedly weaker opponent, the expectation of winning is high. If the opponent is supposedly better than oneself, then the expectation is rather low. Therefore, the probability of a negative emotion occurring is lower if you lose against a stronger opponent than if you lose against a supposedly weak opponent. Expectations also have their effect when they are implicit, i.e., not directly expressed. How intense the emotional reaction is depends not only on expectations but also on the respective consequences.

With *consequences*, we are not talking about real consequences, but always about anticipated emotions, e.g., frustration, shame, pride, that are supposed to arise if the specific case would occur—for example, if one were to lose the close match after all. Anticipated emotions represent the scenarios, e.g., fears, that we are convinced will occur if expectations are not met. In my match against Michael, the consequences of the lost match points were intuitively clear to me: It would be a shame if I missed such an opportunity. I could get a lot of points for the ranking and would regret it if I lost the match after all. But it is also much more serious for the emotional experience that losing a match with a high lead and squandering several match points leads to a loss of self-confidence. The belief in one's own competence to decide the important points in one's favor is massively shaken.

The trigger of an emotion works according to the *principle of association*. If the player comes into the situation again after going through the emotional cycle, the cycle starts from the beginning. In my case, the emotional reaction was triggered every time I had a match point. Even months later, the same reaction occurred in the same situation. This association mechanism contributed to my fear spreading to other, similar situations, such as big points like set balls and break balls. This made my problem even bigger.

*Physical reaction.* Following the trigger, there is always a physical reaction. A few milliseconds after the event, our body reacts to the situation. This reaction is based on very fast evaluations of the situation that are below the threshold of consciousness. Certain regions in the limbic system (i.e., in the amygdala) are activated, which in turn trigger a release of activating hormones. There is a vegetative reaction, which results in an increase in blood pressure, heart rate, muscle tone, and breathing rate. Within a very short time, our body is prepared for a reaction before we are even aware of what is happening. This subconscious mechanism has proven to be useful, even vital, over the course of evolution.

*Action tendencies.* A consequence of the physical reaction is that the person is put into a state of readiness to act. Action tendencies are considered automated patterns of action that are stored in the central nervous system and can be quickly retrieved. The person has one or more action options for each situation, which can then be used. As a rule, the dominant action option prevails, which was used in the past and is considered promising. Such dominant action tendencies do not necessarily have to be implemented, as there is always the possibility to suppress the action tendency if it appears not to be goal-oriented upon closer inspection.

*Emotional expression.* The reaction can be immediately read on the body with careful observation. A dissatisfied facial expression or a loud scream can be an indicator of frustration. A lowered head, drooping shoulders, and a slow walk across the field reflect dejection or despair. A brisk walk with a raised head and broad chest suggests self-confidence and a state of dominance. Body language says more than a thousand words, as it largely involves automated reactions. Voluntary control of physical expression is possible, but requires considerable mental effort. These physical reactions have a direct influence on our subjective experience.

*Subjective impression or feeling.* The physical reactions and the expression of emotion support the development of a subjective impression of the situation and the associated feeling. Vegetative reactions of the body ensure that a subjective impression of the situation is formed, which is usually affectively colored, i.e., positive versus negative. We then have the feeling that things are going well or badly. However, negative feelings weigh much more heavily than positive ones, our well-being and our behavior are much more intensely influenced by negative emotions than by positive ones. A rule of thumb says that three positive events must happen to compensate for the consequences of a negative event on the emotional level (Fredrickson, 2011). This is also the reason why we are often dissatisfied, even when we win. In principle, it is also possible to have an ambiguous feeling when both positive and negative events occur. Especially negative feelings stimulate cognitive processes.

*Higher cognitions.* In this phase of the emotional loop, we become aware of what is going on. We have an impression of whether things are going well or badly. If things are going well, a positive feeling prevails and we focus all our concentration on the next point. But if we are dissatisfied with the course of events, we use cognitive mechanisms to analyze the situation. We try to find out why it is as it is. We look for explanations for the current situation. In doing so, we recall similar and comparable situations from the past from memory and compare them. Due to the fact that events are stored in memory depending on mood, we thus select corresponding positive or negative events. This mechanism further enhances the emotional effect, as memories are retrieved in accordance with the emotional state. Accordingly, we create scenarios for the course of the competition and interpret our own physical and emotional states in terms of their causes. Finally, we initiate measures to regulate our own emotions and body language.

These processes for analyzing the situation and regulating emotions and body language consume considerable cognitive resources, which can affect the player's *concentration*. However, concentration is considered the key to optimal performance in sports. If the player extensively analyzes his situation during a match and constantly goes through various scenarios, he can hardly concentrate on the immediate events.

Lack of concentration leads to a sudden *drop in performance*. This is followed by further negative physical reactions, which reinforce negative emotions and thoughts. The player is now trapped in the cycle of negative emotions. The abrupt drop in performance ensures that the loop of negative emotions continues (Fig. 1.2; Jekauc et al., 2021). The points are lost in

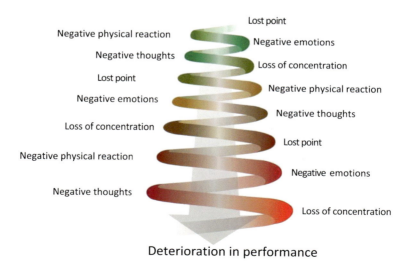

**Fig. 1.2** Downward spiral in the cycle of negative emotions

succession, a victory that was believed to be certain is suddenly given away. The performance stabilizes at a much lower level.

## 1.4 Way Out of the Cycle

Throughout my career, I have repeatedly heard the following sentences: "You just have to concentrate on the next point!", "Stay loose!", "Just be in the here and now!". In theory, these sentences have a lot of truth to them. They outline the way one could manage the cycle of emotions. In practice, however, they remain mere appeals that cannot be realized as such. Once you have fallen into the downward spiral of negative emotions, it is very difficult to get out of it alone. Automated mechanisms, some of which operate below the threshold of consciousness, act like a fast train without brakes. Once they have gained momentum, it is difficult and time-consuming to stop them. Simple appeals and solutions help little in this regard.

To bring the express train of emotions under control, braking systems must be applied at various points in the cycle of emotions (Fig. 1.3; Jekauc et al., 2021). These braking systems, which are called emotion regulation skills, are partly attitudes and partly skills that athletes can acquire through training. Overall, this can be considered a process that is set in motion both through insight and through daily practice.

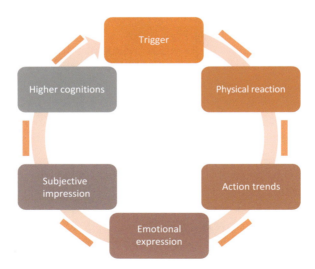

**Fig. 1.3** Slowing down the cycle of emotions

*Neutralize triggers.* The first step in slowing down the cycle is to neutralize the trigger. As already explained, unfavorable outcome expectations and anticipated consequences trigger the cycle of emotions. This involves *identifying and critically reconsidering one's own expectations, values, and attitudes.* If we eliminate the unnecessary burden that leads to the creation of pressure, the emotional reactions will be weaker and will disappear over time.

*Consciously perceive bodily processes.* The next step is to improve perception of one's own body. Only when we are aware of what is happening in our body can we understand ourselves. Physical sensations are a harbinger of our emotional state. Body perception is a skill that can be optimized through exercises.

*Acquisition of favorable action tendencies.* To change action tendencies, they must be reprogrammed. A good strategy for reprogramming action tendencies is imagination training. Here, one imagines a competition situation in a calm environment outside of the competition or training session and mentally goes through one's own action; e.g., after missing a ball, I move from the spot with a determined movement. The more often one imagines the situation and the desired action, the more the action tendency in the situation becomes ingrained.

*Improve body language.* Body perception is a prerequisite for us to also consciously perceive our body language. All emotions manifest themselves in our body, so we can influence our emotional states by improving our body language. Body language not only influences our own well-being, but also affects opponents.

*Manage feelings.* An essential step towards emotional stability relates to dealing with positive and negative feelings. Here, it is also initially about *perceiving one's own feelings.* Only when we succeed in consciously perceiving our own feelings can we consciously deal with them. Every feeling has a meaning that we still need to understand. It is about developing an inner attitude in which we allow and accept our own feelings. Finally, it is about developing strategies to deal with negative feelings and to cultivate positive feelings. As already shown, negative emotions are stronger than positive ones and overall, many more positive feelings are needed to establish emotional balance. Therefore, the cultivation of positive feelings is an essential step towards achieving emotional stability. An important milestone in performance optimization is to remain in emotional balance even under adverse circumstances and in the face of setbacks.

*Build concentration ability.* Concentration ability is considered a key prerequisite for optimal performance in sports. Without concentration, no high performance is possible, regardless of the sport. Concentration is best achieved in a relaxed state and is strongly influenced by emotions. But it is also a prerequisite for other abilities. Without concentration, effective emotion regulation is not possible. We benefit from a strongly developed concentration in a double sense. On the one hand, with good concentration we can better recall performances in competition, on the other hand, we can better regulate our emotions. If the ability to concentrate is strongly developed, then we are also less susceptible to getting caught in a carousel of negative emotions. The good news is that concentration can be trained like a muscle. Visible progress can be achieved after just a few weeks.

## Conclusion

The cycle of emotions can influence our performance in sports like hardly any other phenomenon. If we once get caught in the downward spiral of negative emotions, we can plunge into a deep crisis. A combination of our own performance expectations and anticipated consequences create favorable starting conditions that can set the cycle of emotions in motion. As an athlete, one is under pressure. A deviation from one's own expectations triggers a physical reaction that occurs extremely quickly and below the threshold of consciousness. This reaction is usually immediately recognizable in body posture, gestures, and facial expressions and has an immediate impact on our emotional well-being. The situation is evaluated and an impression is formed about the course of the situation. We have the feeling that things are going well or badly for us. Especially with negative emotions, the state of arousal is much stronger and occupies us more. Causes for the poor course of the competition and one's own physical condition are sought. We recall past experiences, play through scenarios for the future, and prepare strategies for dealing with our own frustrations and negative feelings. Since this preoccupation with oneself requires considerable cognitive resources, the capacities for concentration on the subsequent actions are exhausted. The reduced concentration leads to a decrease in performance, which in turn triggers the emotional chain reaction from the beginning. By going through the emotional loop several times, there is a drastic drop in performance that seems hardly explainable. The performance stabilizes at a significantly lower level.

To break the cycle of emotions, all six components of the cycle must be addressed. Strategies can be applied to each emotion component to achieve emotional stability: 1. Neutralize triggers, 2. Consciously perceive the body, 3. Acquire favorable action tendencies, 4. Improve body language, 5. Manage feelings, and 6. Build concentration ability.

## References

Fredrickson, B. L. (2011). *Die Macht der guten Gefühle*. Campus.

Jekauc, D., Fritsch, J., & Latinjak, A. T. (2021). Toward a theory of emotions in competitive sports. *Frontiers in Psychology, 12,* 790423. https://doi.org/10.3389/fpsyg.2021.790423.

# 2

# History of Mindfulness in Sports

## 2.1 Far Eastern Traditions

The first practices of mindfulness probably date back to Hindu traditions that emerged about 4000 years ago. These are diverse religious practices that are more or less loosely connected to each other[1]. One of the first systematizations of these mindfulness practices and a corresponding doctrine was developed by Siddhartha Gautama, who is also called Buddha. In his search for a way to overcome the suffering and frustrations of life, he discovered that mindfulness is an essential element. In this doctrine, which was developed about 2500 years ago, mindfulness is the first step towards enlightenment. Over time, this doctrine of Buddha formed a religion, which is now referred to as Buddhism.

The teachings of Buddha spread in all directions and reached the area of present-day China in the 6th century. According to legend, the Indian monk Bodhidharma taught the practices of mindfulness in a Shaolin monastery in connection with Shaolin martial arts. While mindfulness and meditation contributed to strengthening the mind, physical exercises were used to strengthen the body. Thus, the Shaolin tradition can be seen as a symbiosis between mental and physical training to improve performance, about

---

[1] Even today, accents of mindfulness can still be recognized in certain forms of yoga. Some mindfulness exercises, such as the body scan exercise, come very close to yoga, as both involve concentration on physical processes. It is suspected that yoga training also improves mindfulness. This assumption was confirmed, for example, by Gaiswinkler and Unterrainer (2016).

© The Author(s), under exclusive license to Springer-Verlag GmbH, DE, part of Springer Nature 2024
D. Jekauc et al., *Mindfulness Training in Sport*,
https://doi.org/10.1007/978-3-662-68804-5_2

1400 years before modern sports psychology was founded in the West. Even today, the Shaolin monks are pushing the boundaries of what is physically possible through meditation and hard training, which is showcased in the West during spectacular performances.

This Buddhist tradition continued to spread eastward towards Korea and Japan, where it took on a new form as Zen. In Zen practice, sitting and walking meditations are often used to maintain a clear consciousness free from suffering and fear. However, the meditative techniques were also extended to other activities, such as archery or gardening. The practitioner immerses himself so deeply in the activity that he forgets himself, completely merges with the task, and perceives a fusion with the activity. This experience of self-forgetfulness, of merging with the task and fusion with the environment, is very similar to the concept of flow in modern psychology, which has a very positive effect on the athlete in sports.

The German philosopher Eugen Herrigel was one of the first to successfully transfer this concept of mindfulness to the West. With his book *ZEN in the Art of Archery* (Herrigel, 1948), he opened up this difficult-to-understand concept in the tradition of Zen Buddhism to a wide audience and explained its significance for the Western cultural sphere. This book was a worldwide success and inspired countless artists, intellectuals, and seekers on the spiritual path—it even inspired American sports educator Timothy Gallwey to write a bestseller.

## 2.2 The Bible of Sports Psychology

Pete Carroll and Steve Kerr are among the most successful coaches in their respective fields, and they have a lot in common. They have similar ideas about how a coach should design training and lead a team. Both were also heavily influenced by the same book during their careers: *The Inner Game of Tennis* by Timothy Gallwey. They always have several copies of it with them to distribute to students who want to further develop their sports psychology skills.

It is astonishing that a book originally written for tennis players and coaches has found such great resonance beyond the tennis scene. Many competitive athletes from various sports still consider it the bible of sports psychology today, several decades after its first publication in 1974. It is estimated that more than a million copies have been sold[2]. This makes it the best-selling tennis book of all time. Due to the wide distribution of his work, American sports educator Gallwey can be considered a pioneer of the mindfulness movement in sports.

Inspired by the Buddhist teachings of Zen, he assumes that every game consists of two parts: an external and an internal part. The athlete plays the external game to win against an external opponent; the internal game, on the other hand, he plays against himself to overcome internal resistances, such as doubts, concentration lapses, nervousness, or self-criticism, and to achieve top performance. The latter is at least as difficult as the external game, as internal resistances can slow us down just as much as strong opponents.

The central thesis of the book is that two types of self exist in every athlete: Self 1 and Self 2 (Gallwey, 1974). Self 1 represents conscious processes in which the person proceeds analytically and tends to ruminate. Self 2, on the other hand, represents rather unconscious and automatic processes that are familiar with the execution of movement. The relationship between these two types of self determines how successful the execution of movement will be. The common problem is that Self 1 repeatedly tries to control the highly automated work processes of Self 2. This leads to tension, loss of coordination, and ultimately a drop in performance in the athlete.

The secret of the inner game is to eliminate the disturbing influences of Self 1, i.e., to eliminate self-critical tendencies. It's about letting Self 2 simply do its thing, without judging or even controlling it. The key to this is focusing on what is happening right now. If Self 1 focuses exclusively on the here and now, it cannot exert any disturbing influences on Self 2. The result is a relaxed and effortless game. The art is to accept the situation without judgment and just let it happen. Gallwey thus introduced the concept of mindfulness as a key to performance optimization, without mentioning this word once in his book. The author recommends practicing meditation exercises and suggests a series of concentration exercises on the court, e.g., focusing on the seam of the ball during a ball exchange. This is intended to train Self 1 to stay in the present.

It is astonishing that Timothy Gallwey proposed a dual process theory long before representatives of scientific psychology. For example, Israeli-American Nobel laureate Daniel Kahneman (2011) assumes, after

---

[2] The English-language news platform BuzzFeed.com estimated in a 2013 article by Reeves Wiedeman that over a million copies of *The Inner Game of Tennis* have been sold.

a multitude of scientific studies[3], that humans have two cognitive systems: One system (System 1) that works automatically, quickly, effortlessly, and without deliberate control, and another system (System 2) that directs attention and is responsible for complex analyses. Thus, today's research seems to confirm Timothy Gallwey's theses. Gallwey's Self 2 would therefore represent the automatic processes of System 1, while Self 1 embodies the conscious processes of System 2. The astonishing thing is that Kahneman only published his book in 2011, i.e., 37 years after Gallwey.

Upon closer inspection, however, it should be emphasized that Gallwey's dual concept, despite great similarities with today's dual process theories, is not entirely compatible. Today's concepts assume that the consciously working system has relatively limited resources available. This often leads to fatigue after prolonged concentrated work. In this state, the automatic and intuitive system takes over, often resulting in thoughtless and impulsive actions. Numerous studies by Kahneman and other scientists show that errors and misjudgments often occur due to the limited activity of the conscious system. Therefore, it is important to properly program and train the conscious system, rather than turning it off.

Gallwey also overlooks the role emotional processes play in athletic performance. Inner resistances such as self-doubt, self-criticism, and lack of self-confidence are now understood more as products of emotional processes and less as the activity of Self 1. According to Gallwey, "destructive self-reflection" is the cause of emotional reactions, not the other way around. Thus, Gallwey's concept aims to treat the consequences rather than the causes. In the first chapter (see Chap. 1), we saw how emotional processes determine our thinking and actions in sports, and in the following chapters, we will learn how to regulate these psychological processes with the help of mindfulness.

In conclusion, it must be stated that Timothy Gallwey was far ahead of his time. Despite simplifying assumptions, he presented a coherent and practical concept from which many useful exercises can be derived. Above all, however, Gallwey paved the way for mindfulness training in sports with this concept.

---

[3] In his book *Thinking, Fast and Slow* from 2011, Daniel Kahneman presents his theory of two cognitive systems. He discusses many studies that support his theses.

## 2.3 Mindfulness Finds Its Way into the NBA

On October 6, 1993, Michael Jordan shocked the basketball world when he announced he was quitting his sport. After his father was brutally murdered in a highway rest stop robbery, the exceptional basketball player decided to end his career at the age of 30. The grief was too great, the emotional hole too deep, to continue as before. He needed time to process his grief. Deep sorrow coupled with the daily pressure that high-performance athletes are exposed to is too much for the human psyche.

The decision to quit basketball was not only hard for him personally, but also for the entire Chicago Bulls team. Michael Jordan was the leading figure of this team. With him, the Bulls won the championship three times in a row, with him contributing the majority of the points. He was not only the playmaker, but also a leadership personality. His sudden withdrawal was a shock to the team. Scottie Pippen, Jordan's longtime teammate and friend, said that the news of his withdrawal felt like his heart had been ripped out of his chest.

This image described the psychological state of the entire team. Phil Jackson, who as coach had won three championships in a row with the Chicago Bulls, felt it was his responsibility to rebuild the team and find an appropriate way to deal with this setback. It was about getting out of this emotional hole and exploiting the existing potential of the team. As history has often taught us, the greatest innovations often emerge from the deepest crises.

In a first step, Jackson tried to incorporate yoga and Tai-Chi into the training—but the resistance in the team was great. Many players complained that everything hurt and they were unable to perform the exercises. None of the players did the exercises voluntarily, so Jackson looked for further alternatives. Eventually, his team contacted George Mumford, a meditation trainer who taught mindfulness practices to patients and prison inmates. As part of a training camp, Mumford introduced the Chicago Bulls players to various mindfulness exercises. This set in motion a process that would fundamentally change the team. The players accepted this new approach to dealing with stress and from then on considered it a fixed part of their training. Step by step, Mumford succeeded in establishing mindfulness training as an integral part of their training regimen.

Phil Jackson understood that the team had a competitive advantage over other NBA teams through the use of mindfulness training. This allowed him to pull certain levers to stabilize team performance and influence how quickly they recovered from difficult losses. Over time, the players learned to accept the situation as it is and not to quarrel too much with themselves and teammates. Little by little, they developed a certain serenity in dealing with themselves and others. The players focused more on the process of performance in the here and now than on the result itself. This detachment from focusing on the result prevented pressure and fear from arising and freed up additional resources.

The consequence of such an attitude towards one's own profession was the renewed joy in the sport. Suddenly, it was fun to play basketball again. Instead of dealing with the consequences of their own actions and past defeats, the players increasingly focused on what was happening right now. The effects of the training sessions now had a stronger impact on the upcoming matches. The team worked purposefully and consistently on their plan and were less often distracted by the circumstances of the situation.

Although most experts only gave the Chicago Bulls outsider chances without Michael Jordan and hardly anyone trusted them to make it to the playoffs, the team did surprisingly well. In the first half of the regular season, their performances fluctuated greatly, but the team was always able to overcome their weak phases and put together several series of seven or ten wins in a row. Eventually, the Jackson team qualified for the playoffs. There, they confidently mastered the first round against the Cleveland Cavaliers with a 3:0 win. In the second round of the playoffs, the team only narrowly lost 4:3 to the New York Knicks after a great fight. Jackson continued his collaboration with George Mumford over the years, secured three more NBA titles with the Chicago Bulls, and won five more NBA titles with the Los Angeles Lakers. Today, Jackson, with a total of eleven titles, is considered the most successful coach in NBA history.

Mindfulness training is certainly not the sole reason for Jackson's success story. However, it is one of many mosaic pieces that need to come together to achieve great success. Especially in difficult situations, it is important to remain calm and maintain focus on the essentials. In absolute top-level sports, the performance differences are very small and so such small things can make the difference between victory and defeat. Although everyone knows how important mental strength is, the path to achieving it is hardly known and involves considerable training effort. Phil Jackson recognized the potential of mindfulness training and integrated it into his training operation.

The path that Phil Jackson took in the 1990s has left a lasting impression on the American basketball world. Some NBA greats report having greatly benefited from mindfulness training. For example, Kobe Bryant, a former player of Phil Jackson, repeatedly emphasized in interviews during his time with the Los Angeles Lakers how important mindfulness was for him and that he regularly practiced mindfulness exercises. Over the years, he developed the ability to maintain his concentration in the here and now for longer periods of time and to remain calm regardless of the score. Bryant was considered one of the mentally strongest basketball players in the world during his career. In decisive phases of the matches, he repeatedly demonstrated a steady hand and brought his team important victories. In heated phases of the matches, he did not let opponents provoke him and remained calm even in the face of obvious hostilities. He described George Mumford, who had opened the way to mindfulness for him, as one of the most influential people in his life.

## 2.4  The Legacy of Phil Jackson

As we have seen, Phil Jackson introduced mindfulness training in basketball in the early 1990s. One person who has further developed the concept of mindfulness in basketball is Steve Kerr. In his career as a basketball player, Kerr played under Phil Jackson for the Chicago Bulls between 1993 and 1998, where he first experienced mindfulness. During this golden era of the Chicago Bulls, in which they won three NBA championships, Steve Kerr developed into one of the NBA's best distance shooters. He still holds the record for the highest three-point percentage over his entire career (shooting percentage 45.4%). After the end of his active career as a professional player, he worked as a basketball television expert and as a manager for the Phoenix Suns. Eventually, he decided to continue his career as a coach.

After there had been major quarrels and disruptions in the club's management, Kerr took over the position of head coach of the Golden State Warriors in May 2014. The team had played a rather subordinate role in the NBA in the preceding decades. Their last title was 39 years ago, although the team had reached the playoffs the year before Kerr's engagement. The task of Steve Kerr to bring calm back to the club and build a functioning team was not easy under these conditions. The inexperienced coach, as one of his first official acts, took a trip to Seattle to shadow Pete Caroll, the football coach of the Seahawks, at training camp. Carroll already had a 40-year career as a football coach at that time and was known for his good rapport with his players. In Seattle, Steve Kerr was to gain important experiences that influenced his leadership style and his entire career as a basketball coach. Carroll asked him the seemingly simple question of how he wants to coach his team.

Essentially, he wanted to find out what team culture Kerr wanted to establish and how he wanted to lead his team.

On that day, the former basketball player reflected on his entire career and the lessons he had learned from Phil Jackson at the Chicago Bulls and from Gregg Popovich at the San Antonio Spurs. From a mix of his own ideas and his experiences, Kerr eventually developed a coaching concept with four guiding principles that were to make up the DNA of the Golden State Warriors in the coming years. The goal of this concept was to create conditions under which young, talented players could develop into world-class players. The four core principles include: joy, mindfulness, compassion, and competition.

*Joy.* Truly good performance can only be achieved when there is a positive mood in the team. Joy is the emotional opposite of fear and pressure. If you enjoy the game, you can overcome inevitable phases of the season when things are not going so well more quickly. However, joy usually does not come on its own, but must be prepared. Steve Kerr's goal is for his team to have fun in every training session and competition. Therefore, he works day by day with his coaching team to incorporate elements of humor and bring a good mood into training. For this, he has developed a whole range of measures with videos, music, personal actions, etc.

*Mindfulness.* To cope with the adversities of tough professional sports, mindfulness plays an important role. If we manage to stay present in the here and now and consciously experience the moment, the risk of falling into emotional lows decreases. Emotional setbacks are an integral part of professional sports, but it is always important to remember that life is bigger than successes and failures in sports. Taking a step back and looking at the overall situation of life with a bit of distance can help to focus on the essentials. To advance this process, Kerr has commissioned a meditation trainer to offer mindfulness sessions at regular intervals. In addition, the players have the opportunity to work on an individual level in this area.

*Compassion.* The interest in what moves the players and the knowledge of how tough the business in professional basketball is and what sacrifices the players have to make is the product of a characteristic called compassion or empathy. At first glance, the life of a professional basketball player seems like a fairy tale in which the players earn many millions of dollars for something they love to do anyway. However, this assessment often overlooks adversities such as serious injuries, fears, pressure situations, family burdens, and open hostilities. To advance the players also on a human level, a coach must open up to such aspects. It is also his task to promote compassion among the athletes so that they can support each other in difficult situations. Small gestures like high-fiving or cheering despite mistakes can contribute to the development of a real team spirit. If a player knows that the coaching team and his teammates stand behind him no matter what happens, then he can dare to push his own performance limits without fearing failure.

*Competition.* Competition is the central characteristic of competitive sports and is often at the top of the hierarchy of values in many teams. In Steve Kerr's conception, this principle is deliberately not at the top, as it is already present. Kerr's aim is to accept the competition and develop a healthy attitude towards it. In training, competitive situations are created, which increases the appeal of training and simulates the real competition situation. The players learn to constantly put their own performances to the test and receive feedback on what they can work on to further develop themselves.

Against the backdrop of these four guiding principles, Steve Kerr designed every single training session and every preparation for a match from the very beginning. First, he managed to convey these values to his own coaching team. Gradually, the entire team also opened up to this philosophy. Under these conditions, players like Andre Iguodala, Klay Thompson, Draymond Green, or Stephen Curry experienced unexpected development spurts that elevated the team's game to a new level. Steve Kerr had a dream start to his first season as coach of the Golden State Warriors. Of the first 23 games, his team won 21, something that had never been achieved by any other coach in his first season in NBA history. The team rushed from victory to victory, ended the regular season with 67–15, and thus confidently qualified for the playoffs. Also there, the team shone from the first round to the final, where the Golden State Warriors recorded four victories out of six games against the Cleveland Cavaliers and thus won their first title in 40 years.

This success of the Golden State Warriors was not a one-time process in which the team had played themselves into a frenzy and had grown beyond themselves. Rather, it can be assumed that it was a sustainable and stable development. In the following years, the team played at a comparable level. In the 2015/16 season, the team again confidently reached the final of the playoffs, in which they narrowly lost in the seventh game with 89 to 93 against the Cleveland Cavaliers. In the following two years, the Golden State Warriors again won the NBA championship and confirmed their class.

Steve Kerr has managed with his four-component concept to develop a solid team into an outstanding team. He has created conditions under which young players can develop optimally. However, the development of game philosophies is not a unique feature of Steve Kerr. Most coaches in professional sports now work with elaborated concepts when taking over teams. Often, however, game-related or tactical aspects are in the foreground, less so psychological ones.

The innovative aspect of this four-component concept is that it emphasizes emotional factors such as joy in sports, mindfulness, and compassion. While older generations of coaches often saw joy in the game as a weakness and unprofessional attitude, psychological research today assumes that positive emotions are a prerequisite for intrinsic motivation. Without joy in sports, it is hardly possible to train long-term and highly motivated at a high level. From this perspective, the motivation of the players is not only dependent on their individual attitude, but also on characteristics of the training. The way the training is designed can promote or undermine motivational potentials. Perhaps the rapid development spurt within the Golden State Warriors team can be attributed to such motivational potentials.

As we will see in subsequent chapters, mindfulness training can contribute to dealing with one's own emotions. Focusing one's own concentration on the present moment can help to consciously perceive one's own emotional states, which usually occur automatically, and to deal with them. It is assumed that mindfulness training can reduce the use of dysfunctional emotion regulation strategies, which favors rapid recovery after emotional setbacks. Overall, successful teams are characterized by a certain emotional stability.

Another innovation of this concept is to address compassion as a crucial control variable of interpersonal relationships. If this is highly developed within the team, members of a team can exchange messages much more effectively. If the team members feel that the others are interested in their well-being, mutual sympathy can also develop. In this way, conditions are created under which the cohesion between the team members can be strengthened. Especially in stressful situations, such soft factors matter.

Finally, at the center of this approach is not the result, but the development of the players. No goals are set that the team should have achieved by the end of the year, but rather processes are stimulated that promote the development of the players. The players are also aware of this fact, which can arouse acceptance and enthusiasm on the part of the players. From such development-promoting conditions, joy in the game is more likely to arise than the fear of failure.

## 2.5 A Man with Nerves of Steel

It's the semi-final of Doha 2017. Novak Djokovic takes the lead in the first set against Fernando Verdasco, who is ranked 42nd in the world at the time. At one point, the score is 4:2, unsurprisingly. But suddenly Verdasco catches up. The game turns. Djokovic actually loses the first set 4:6. Then the second set, it's close, it comes to a tiebreak. With a mini-break, Djokovic again gets off to a better start at 2:1. But then—as in the first set—the barely conceivable happens. He gives up five points in a row, three on his own and two on the opponent's serve. Again, he fails to close the deal and bring his lead home. A few minor mistakes, the determined play of his opponent—and suddenly Djokovic is on the brink of defeat. Now he has four match points against him. Can he still turn this match around?

With the self-inflicted defeat in sight, it would be quite normal to be frustrated. But Djokovic doesn't seem frustrated or nervous at all. Rather, he gives a calm but determined impression. He fends off the first match point with a good serve and a bravely played attack ball. With a bit of luck, a lot of playing ability, and because his opponent is getting more and more nervous, Djokovic manages to win the tiebreak 9:7 after all. In the third set, Verdasco is visibly affected. He doesn't seem as nervous as in the tiebreak, but his concentrated tension has noticeably decreased. Unlike in the games before, he no longer cheers himself on. It seems only a matter of time before Verdasco gives in. At 2:2, Djokovic actually manages the break and Verdasco's resistance is broken. In the end, Djokovic wins the third and decisive set 6:3.

Novak Djokovic has once again managed to win a match that was thought to be lost. From his perspective, it was not a good match in terms of gameplay. He made some avoidable mistakes and did not take advantage of several opportunities in the first and second set. Despite these missed opportunities and the seemingly insurmountable deficit, he remained quite calm even in difficult phases. On the other hand, Verdasco appeared nervous at crucial points in the tiebreak and was downcast after the missed match points. His body language revealed clear signs of frustration and, at times, resignation after each mistake. As a spectator, it is quite understandable how Verdasco must have felt. Probably a thousand thoughts went through his head, such as: Why didn't I take my chances? If only I had played a bit more boldly, if only I had taken a riskier serve or played the forehand with a bit more spin! Probably each of us would have felt like Verdasco if we had been so close to a major victory. However, the question is whether this brooding and self-doubt makes the difference between one of the greatest players in tennis history and a very solid tennis professional.

Because Djokovic found himself in a similar situation at the ATP tournament in Monte Carlo in April 2018, when he could not convert nine match points against Borna Coric. Several match points got stuck at the net edge, one ball bounced just a few millimeters out. Probably each of us would have been desperate. Some would have thrown their racket, others would have tried to swallow their frustration, and many would have complained about their lack of luck or inability, or attacked the referee for an unfavorable decision. These are all human reactions when we are frustrated.

Novak Djokovic, however, reacted quite differently at this tournament. He did not seem frustrated at all. His posture was upright, his stride evenly fast, his gaze steady and focused. There were no signs that he was nervous, irritated, or frustrated. He appeared calm. Eventually, Djokovic calmly converted the tenth match point and narrowly won the match 7:6, 7:5.

The list of such situations in which Djokovic remains calm and wins despite high pressure is very long. It seems that this calmness and composure in tight and decisive match situations are his strength. Under-pressure statistics from the ATP portal show that Djokovic has the best odds in decisive game situations[4]. When considering this world ranking statistic over his entire career, he leads it and even leaves behind the legendary Pete Sampras, who was considered the most composed and coolest player in the world during his career. Ranked Third and Fourth are Rafael Nadal and Roger Federer, the most successful players in tennis history.

The question now arises as to where Djokovic gets the positive energy to leave such setbacks behind so easily. Where does the composure in dealing with his own mistakes come from? How does he manage not to slide into negativity? How does he manage to maintain his concentration in nerve-wracking situations?

How important it is for him to maintain his emotional balance, he explained in his book *Serve to win* first published in 2013 and in numerous interviews. In his eyes, our fears are our greatest enemies. If he had allowed his fears to take away his confidence, he would never have reached the top of the world. He works every day to keep his emotional state in balance. He focuses on the following three points:

---

[4] The under-pressure statistic takes into account four parameters that often represent the decisive situations in the match: 1) the percentage of break points won, 2) the percentage of break points defended, 3) the percentage of tiebreaks won, and 4) the percentage of decisive sets won.

## 2  History of Mindfulness in Sports    29

*Mindfulness.* One of the great secrets of Djokovic's success is his ability to quickly recover from emotional setbacks. This enables him to immediately let go of mistakes and be fully present for the next point. He relies on mindfulness, i.e., he focuses on the present moment without judging it. He registers and accepts all emerging thoughts and feelings. No matter how negative and disadvantageous they may be, he does not try to control, fight, or suppress them. Every moment, every physical and mental state is accepted, with the focus remaining on the present moment. Consistently implemented, such an approach ensures an inner state of equanimity towards one's own mistakes and mishaps, acting like an emotional shield. All adversities of the game bounce off Djokovic, hardly leading to an emotional reaction. Djokovic has not always possessed this ability to deal calmly with himself and his own mistakes. Only through regular training has he managed to apply this mindful state also in tennis matches. In his book *Serve To Win*, he describes what this looks like in practice:

"How do I manage not to let my 'lows' drag me down? It's due to the way I think—or at least try to think. It doesn't always work under all circumstances. But when it does, it works wonders. Psychologists call it 'mindfulness'. [...] I do this exercise for about 15 minutes every day. It gives me clarity and is as important to me as my physical training. [...] I used to waste a lot of energy and time on my 'inner battles', or whatever you want to call it, and lost sight of what was happening around me, what was happening in the moment [...] I used to freeze when I made a mistake, and was convinced that I wasn't playing in the same league as the Federers and Andy Murrays of this world. When I mess up a serve or a backhand today, the self-doubts still come up briefly, but I now know how to deal with them: I acknowledge the negative thoughts, let them go and focus on the moment. This mindfulness also helps me deal with pain and emotions. It helps me focus on what's really important and quiet my thoughts. This is particularly useful in the middle of a Grand Slam final." (Djokovic, 2015, p. 102 f.). *quote translated from German*

*Nutrition.* To achieve physical and emotional well-being, nutrition plays a prominent role. A large part of the emotional processes are processed in the gastrointestinal region. Disturbances in this region massively influence physical and mental processes. In 2010, Djokovic was diagnosed with gluten intolerance, which often robbed him of physical and mental reserves in important match phases. Through a radical change in diet, Djokovic was able to exploit his physical and psychological potentials much better, which had a massive impact on his performance. Before the dietary change, he had to give up some matches due to exhaustion. Djokovic is now considered one of the fittest players on the tour. Therefore, a diet adapted to individual needs is a prerequisite for physical and emotional stability in sports. Djokovic has since published his dietary concepts and gives advice on how athletes should eat properly.

*Social Network.* An important pillar in Novak Djokovic's life is his family and friends. They provide him with support and help him find his emotional balance. When he gets into difficult situations, where he is under pressure and exposed to stress, social support has a balancing effect for him. His motto is: "You are who you surround yourself with". He has therefore surrounded himself with people who believe in him and with whose help he has become what he is today. He always has his family and his team, now all friends, around him. They experience all the highs and lows of a professional tennis player's everyday life together. Although tennis is an individual sport, a player's top performance can only be a team effort. Each member of the team performs their task in harmonious coordination with the others. A social network has emerged that optimally serves Djokovic's emotional needs and repeatedly creates the conditions for top performance.

## 2.6 A Leap to Greater Inner Strength

She has worked hard for a large part of her life to achieve her dream of Olympic gold. Now, here in Tokyo, she has one last chance to realize this dream today. In many Olympic disciplines, it comes down to a few moments when you have to call upon your best performance. A sprinter must throw all her energy and skill into the balance in the final race to outrun her competitors. A long jumper has only a few attempts to show the best jump. Otherwise, the years of effort will not be crowned with the gold medal. Of course, she has already come very far and won gold at both the European and World Championships. But basically, few people are interested in how well you did in training and what performances you showed in other competitions. Now it's all about this one moment. There is also a lot of money at stake, every athlete who has made sport their profession knows that. A great burden of Olympic sports is to withstand this pressure, this knowledge of what is at stake and what is at risk, and not to tense up.

Malaika Mihambo has already made five attempts. One remains, the sixth and thus final jump into the sandpit of Tokyo. And it has to be right, it has to approach seven meters if the color of the medal is to be gold in the end. Two competitors had jumped two centimeters further than Malaika Mihambo in the previous attempts, so she has to take the lead in the last attempt. Six meters ninety-seven needs to be surpassed. At the Olympic Games in Rio in 2016, she finished fourth and narrowly missed a medal. Will she jump past the medals again this time?

No, now Malaika Mihambo is fully there and actually manages to reach the seven-meter mark with her last jump. Her two competitors can still catch up, but in the end, they do not manage to surpass Mihambo's seven-meter mark with their last jump. When everything comes down to the last attempt, the competitors can still catch up afterwards, the whole long jump world revolves only around this one jump and nothing less than Olympic gold is at stake, how does Malaika Mihambo manage not to break under the pressure? How does she manage to run up, jump off and despite not even hitting the board, achieve an outstanding distance of exactly seven meters? How does she manage to jump past her competitors by three centimeters in the very last attempt? How does she manage to win gold?

Looking back: Athletics World Championship, Doha 2019. After an invalid attempt in the second round, everything came to a head for long jumper Malaika Mihambo in this competition as well. The third jump had to be right. An incredible pressure situation, here too it was about gold, here too everything depended on the next jump. And what did Malaika Mihambo do in this exceptional moment? She sat down and meditated. She took a moment for herself. Her mindfulness leads her to notice when she is under pressure, to detect shallow breathing and to be sensitized when the run-up is not right. And in Doha, she was under pressure, hence the meditation. She let go of the negative thoughts, fully immersed herself in the moment here and now, left the pressure behind and only saw the run-up in front of her. Nothing else mattered more than this moment and the next jump. It was to be a leap to gold, a leap to seven meters thirty, world-class.

Malaika Mihambo will later say about the moments before her Olympic gold jump in Tokyo that she focused on her inner strength. That she started running calmly and confidently because she could be satisfied with this mental strength. And this despite the fact that the jumps on the way to Tokyo were rather mixed, as she had to struggle with a change in her run-up. But instead of slowing herself down too much with self-doubts, she kept getting up from the sandpit and telling herself that she can do it.

For Malaika Mihambo, meditation is not something spiritual, as she focuses on mental aspects rather than religious ones. She gets to know herself in meditation, can reflect and switch off. This gives her the opportunity to be so free in her mind that she can focus on the essentials, on the next jump, on the current training week, on the moment. This is how she manages to make the best of the current situation, the moment here and now.

An important support in this is her breath. When she focuses on her breathing, her body can calm down, her heartbeat slows down. By calming the body, her thoughts also become calmer, which she can then block out. This mental strength, this inner serenity, is Malaika Mihambo's path to gold.

## 2.7 Effects of Mindfulness Training in Competitive and Elite Sports

As we have seen in Chap. 1, in competitive sports, one is always susceptible to getting caught in the whirlpool of the cycle of emotions. Once we get into this cycle, it is extremely difficult to get out. A process is set in motion that can partly not be controlled voluntarily and that has a massive influence on our performance. The constant pressure to perform, personal expectations and the expectations of others provide an optimal ground for the development of these emotional processes. Once the emotional processes have started, they are hard to stop. They develop a dynamic of their own that has the effect of a fast train without brakes.

Nevertheless, a number of athletes have managed to get this cycle of emotions under control and use it productively for competitive sports through mindfulness training. As has already been demonstrated, some top athletes used or use mindfulness training to optimize their performance. Regular mindfulness training has also changed the personality of these athletes. Some new characteristics and competencies have developed, which are very likely not innate, but shaped by life circumstances. Some neurophysiological studies suggest that mindfulness training alters the structures of the brain that underlie these changes in personality. Leading the way are the working group around the American neuroscientist Prof. Dr. Richard Davidson from the University of Wisconsin-Madison (Davidson & Begley, 2012) and the German psychologist Dr. Britta Hölzel from the Technical University of Munich (Hölzel & Brähler, 2015) who have shown that mindfulness training results in changes in certain brain areas associated with concentration and emotion regulation.

In relation to competitive sports, the question arises as to what characteristics and competencies athletes have acquired through mindfulness training that help them cope with performance pressure. Although each sport has its own rules and psychological requirements, at least four general psychological skills can be mentioned that contribute to a productive handling of pressure.

1. *Serenity.* To maintain both health and performance in sports in the long or short term, a certain degree of emotional balance is a necessary prerequisite. Although emotionality and passion are performance-enhancing in some phases of competition, it is always necessary to return to a state of calm and balance after a certain time. The key to returning to this state time and again is *serenity.* In some phases of competition, events may overlap, unexpected occurrences may occur, and it is precisely in these phases that it is important to remain calm and maintain composure. This always sounds easy in theory, but in practice it is not so easy to implement. Fortunately, serenity can be trained to a certain degree.

2. *Resilience.* To be successful in competitive sports, it is not only about celebrating great victories, but also about coping with bitter defeats and overcoming setbacks. A tennis player may make a simple mistake at an important point or a footballer may miss an important penalty, but it is important to quickly put these setbacks behind and look forward. If, on the other hand, one stays too long in this emotional low and deals with the failure for weeks and months, it becomes increasingly difficult to get out of the performance hole. The doubts will definitely not decrease. Djokovic very aptly described that his emotional lows have not become as deep through mindfulness training and he can more easily shake off setbacks. A condition for gaining this resilience is to adopt an inner attitude of not judging things and accepting them as they are. This sounds very logical and simple in theory, but in practice it means a long process of change until one is able to consistently apply this attitude.

3. *Resource management.* Another competency necessary to achieve peak performance in sports is the optimal management of one's own resources. These resources refer to both physical and psychological reserves that are necessary for performance. For example, a marathon runner has only a limited amount of physical resources to cope with the marathon run and she must allocate her resources accordingly to achieve the best possible time. A football player also has to manage his resources when deciding how hard to go into duels. If he goes too hard into the duels, he risks injuring himself or the opponent and getting a red card, if he acts too cautiously, he will lose most of the duels. The same applies to psychological resources. A table tennis player has to decide how often and how intensely she pushes herself in a match. If she pushes herself too often and very intensely, she may not have enough energy in the decisive phases at the end of the match to throw everything into the balance. If she pushes

herself too little or not at all, she can fall into a mental state of defensiveness and passivity, in which she is no longer able to mobilize all her forces. Resource management is therefore about correctly assessing one's own resources and developing a strategy for the optimal use of these resources. This competency requires a good self-perception of physical and psychological processes.

4. *Concentration.* As we have already seen in Chap. 1, concentration is the central psychological resource necessary for the best performance in many sports. Loss of concentration is often associated with severe performance breakdowns. As a psychological resource, concentration also has a limited capacity, which can be exhausted during a competition. When this resource is exhausted, the phenomenon of *Ego Depletion* occurs, in which we often make careless mistakes (Baumeister et al., 2000). One consequence of this is that we always have to take breaks in order to be able to fully use this psychological resource in important phases of the competition. The good news is that the capacity for concentration increases over the course of an athlete's career, i.e., over the course of a career, we are increasingly able to concentrate optimally. The second piece of good news is that this ability can be systematically trained and improved from adolescence onwards.

Based on these four skills, mindfulness training promotes various competencies that are necessary for controlling and optimizing performance. Our mindfulness program will be presented in the next chapter.

# References

Baumeister, R. F., Muraven, M., & Tice, D. M. (2000). Ego depletion: A resource model of volition, self-regulation, and controlled processing. *Social Cognition, 18*(2), 130–150. https://doi.org/10.1521/soco.2000.18.2.130.

Davidson, R. J., & Begley, S. (2012). *The emotional life of your brain: How its unique patterns affect the way you think, feel, and live—and how you can change them*. Hudson Street Press.

Djokovic, N. (2015). *Siegernahrung. Glutenfreie Ernährung für Höchstleistung*. Riva Verlag.

Gaiswinkler, L., & Unterrainer, H. F. (2016). The relationship between yoga involvement, mindfulness and psychological well-being. *Complementary Therapies in Medicine, 26,* 123–127. https://doi.org/10.1016/j.ctim.2016.03.011.

Gallwey, T. (1974). *The inner game of tennis*. Random House.

Herrigel, E. (1948). *Zen in der Kunst des Bogenschießens*. Weller.

Hölzel, B., & Brähler, C. (Eds.). (2015). *Achtsamkeit mitten im Leben. Anwendungsgebiete und wissenschaftliche Perspektiven*. OW Barth.

Kahneman, D. (2011). *Thinking, fast and slow*. Macmillan.

# Part II
# The Program

# 3

# The Mindfulness Program for Athletes

## 3.1 Principles of Mindfulness Training in Sports

Building on considerations about the psychological demands in competitive sports and the processes of the cycle of emotions, our mindfulness training is based on five principles: value awareness, perception of one's own body and thoughts, awareness of one's own impact, acceptance of one's own feelings and thoughts, and focus on what is happening right now. In Fig. 3.1, the five principles of mindfulness training are presented.

*Value Awareness.* The starting point of every emotional surge are our values, expectations, and self-defined standards. If there is a deviation from these values, positive or negative affective states are triggered, which can culminate in a fully developed emotion. If our values, expectations, and standards are met or significantly exceeded, e.g., by leading against a much higher-ranked team, positive affective states occur. In the case of negative deviations, e.g., by falling behind against a lower-ranked opponent, negative affective states occur. Our values not only refer to performance-related standards (e.g., winning against weaker opponents), but also general value attitudes, such as fairness, honesty, discipline, fun, etc. If someone violates these standards, emotionally induced conflicts can occur. Often, however, we are not even aware of our values and expectations, even though they massively influence our emotional well-being. It can happen that we get very upset in training or competition and we can't even say exactly why. In many

© The Author(s), under exclusive license to Springer-Verlag GmbH, DE, part of Springer Nature 2024
D. Jekauc et al., *Mindfulness Training in Sport*,
https://doi.org/10.1007/978-3-662-68804-5_3

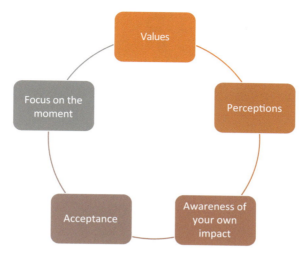

Fig. 3.1 Principles of Mindfulness Training

cases, we adopt value attitudes and expectations from our parents, friends, or coaches without dealing with the meaningfulness of these values. Therefore, an important component of our program is the creation of awareness for one's own values. Only when we are aware of our own values can we understand our feelings.

*Perception.* Perception plays an important role in mindfulness training, as a large part of our inner states is not conscious to us. Many tasks and activities are done automatically and not critically questioned, even if they are no longer functional. We do many things that are not good for us. In many cases, we do not feel important body signals, e.g., back pain, and only realize how we are doing when it may be too late and a permanent injury has occurred. To even notice what is going on inside us and what is good for us, a differentiated perception of our inner processes is essential. This perception refers to both physical and thought aspects. Therefore, a large part of mindfulness training is used to consciously perceive one's own physical sensations and thoughts. An important step towards more mindfulness is becoming aware of one's own physical sensations and thoughts, which usually occur automatically and unconsciously. Only when we are aware of these physical processes and thoughts can we react to them in a targeted and deliberate manner.

*Awareness of One's Own Impact.* A relatively large part of communication takes place non-verbally and below the threshold of consciousness. Like an iceberg, only a small part is above the surface, while the majority is not visible. Only a small part of the transmitted message is consciously perceived and processed. The transmission of our own emotional states takes place in relatively old parts of the brain in terms of evolutionary history and occurs unconsciously. Body language is probably the oldest language in the world and is understood by most mammals. Accordingly, the way we experience and express our emotions is perceived by others. Some sports psychological studies show that our body language influences both teammates and opponents (see Furley & Schweizer, 2020). We can intimidate or build up our opponents, depending on how we react to certain situations. One goal of mindfulness training is to become aware of one's own body language and reflect on it.

*Acceptance.* All people have a common tendency to seek the positive and avoid the negative. However, in sports, it is often the case that negative events cannot be avoided. In most sports, the constant failure in the sense that something does not succeed is the central aspect of the sport. Resisting the inevitable can cost us a lot of energy, which we might lack later in the competition. A very important lesson on the way to an emotionally stable athlete is the ability to accept unpleasant situations and take up the challenge. This also includes facing one's own feelings and not suppressing them. For example, the first step to overcoming one's own fear is to first accept the fear and not fight it. Because when we start to fight certain emotions, their effect only becomes stronger. Therefore, a central goal of mindfulness training is to adopt an attitude of acceptance towards oneself but also towards others.

*Focus on the moment.* One of the central aspects of mindfulness training is the concentration on what is happening in the moment. When we are in the present, we cannot dwell on negative thoughts, which gives us a certain emotional stability. Concentration is a prerequisite for all processes we want to perform consciously. As a beginner in mindfulness training, one repeatedly realizes how difficult it is to keep the concentration on one point and we constantly drift off in thoughts. A large part of our efforts in mindfulness training will initially be to train our ability to concentrate. Many exercises will only succeed when a sufficient level of concentration is present. Therefore, it is important to constantly bring the focus back to the point and notice the distraction. With increasing training, our ability to concentrate will also improve.

## 3.2 What is Mindfulness and How Does it Work?

Mindfulness is hocus pocus, something spiritual that only religious people practice to meditate—this could be a prejudice that comes to mind when thinking of mindfulness. But the fact that mindfulness is effective and proves to be a real problem solver is no longer a secret in science: Mindfulness-based training can reduce the symptoms of stress, anxiety, and depression and help to deal more effectively with emotions. So if, as in Chap. 1, it is about escaping the cycle of negative emotions, balancing emotions, and building concentration, then the step towards mindfulness is not far off.

Mindfulness is about directing the focus of one's attention to the immediate experience in the here and now and consciously perceiving this experience, but not evaluating it. Feelings that arise, thoughts that shoot through the head, perceptions that occur, are registered, but not immediately classified as disturbing or hindering. It becomes intuitively clear that the absence of evaluation and the acceptance of one's own state are brakes in the emotional cycle. If one realizes that the cycle of emotions can lead to a drastic drop in performance when run through multiple times, mindfulness, with its potential to escape the cycle, represents an option for performance enhancement. Overall, three mechanisms of action of mindfulness, which are still relatively little researched in the sports context, are assumed to explain the relationship between mindfulness and performance improvement: more flow, improved concentration, and more effective emotion regulation (Jekauc & Kittler, 2015).

*Flow.* Whether at work, doing household chores, or playing sports: We know the impression of being fully in the *flow* from various fields of activity. A flow theory was developed by the psychologist Mihály Csikszentmihalyi (1990) and made popular in psychology. Today, flow is a well-researched phenomenon in sports psychology. It occurs especially when the challenges that the situation presents to us and the abilities that we can counter these challenges with are in balance, i.e., when there is no over- or under-demand, but the situation fits exactly to our own performance. Suddenly we perceive nothing around us, dive in, are so immersed in the task that all worries or other concerns seem forgotten. The concept of flow describes this state of highest concentration and complete immersion in an activity. Where there is no room for doubt, where negative thoughts have no chance, where body and mind are in harmony, a good feeling arises and performance is optimal.

Thus, mindfulness and flow are similar, especially in that only the moment in the here and now is perceived and the concentration is entirely directed at the immediate task. It is therefore not surprising that mindfulness-based programs can also increase the level of flow state. The assumption behind this mechanism of action is that mindfulness training can contribute to the occurrence of flow and this then has a positive effect on performance.

*Concentration.* To achieve the best performance in sports, optimal attention is required. This can be determined by four facets of attention. The focus of attention should not be so broad that all, actually irrelevant impressions are perceived and act as a distraction. Such disturbing factors, such as an announcement by the stadium announcer directed at the fans, should simply be able to be blocked out, which is referred to as selective attention. In football, a game lasts 90 min and accordingly, the player should still be able to perceive what is happening on the field in the ninetieth min. This ability for sustained attention allows the attention to be maintained throughout the entire length of the competition (if necessary until the penalty shootout). In addition, orienting attention is required, which is about the deliberately controllable direction of attention in space, i.e., being able to target and understand relevant stimuli from the environment. The fourth aspect is divided attention, which includes a certain flexibility that allows one to focus on the ball one moment and the opponent the next, i.e., to shift attention from one stimulus to another. All these aspects of attention could be related to mindfulness, so the assumption behind the second mechanism of action. After all, mindfulness is all about directing attention in a certain direction, such as one's own breath and especially the immediate moment. In fact, studies have found that mindfulness training is associated with an improvement in the four mentioned facets of attention. If attention can be trained through mindfulness, i.e., if the ability to concentrate can be improved, this could explain why performance also increases as a result.

*Emotion regulation.* The third mechanism of action lies in the already outlined emotion regulation. Mindfulness is not necessarily about eliminating negative emotions and promoting positive ones. Because this is not really possible: if one consciously tries not to fall into fear, it is likely to happen even more. Rather, mindfulness should also perceive potentially obstructive states and not suppress them from the outset. They should simply not be evaluated, the focus should always be brought back to the here and now after an inevitable wandering of thoughts. The negative emotion is thus deprived of its foundations, namely the evaluation of the trigger and the cognitions associated with it, which weakens it in the long term. For example, if competition anxiety is accepted and not suppressed, it loses its threat. It no longer appears as an oversized opponent against whom one can only lose and should therefore avoid. Instead, it is accepted that the fear is there, which opens up completely new possibilities, e.g. that one uses the fear to one's advantage. Thus, fear becomes an ally instead of an opponent. Research indeed suggests that there is a correlation between mindfulness and competition optimism, while competition anxiety is less pronounced when mindfulness has been trained. The improved performance could then be associated with the improved emotion regulation achieved through mindfulness.

## 3.3 Development of the Program

When I (Darko Jekauc) read the newly published book "The emotional life of your brain" by Richard Davidson and Sharon Begley 2012, which introduced emotional styles and meditation techniques, I immediately realized the potential that mindfulness training could have in sports. Richard Davidson is a renowned neuroscientist who has extensively dealt with the topic of emotions and emotion regulation in the brain. In numerous works, he and his team were able to show that practicing mindfulness leads to structural changes in the brain that are important for resilience, perception of emotions, or concentration, among other things. The scientific evidence clearly pointed in the direction that various mindfulness practices could positively influence these characteristics, which are of high importance from a sports psychology perspective. I decided to sign up for a meditation course right away. At the University of Konstanz, where I was then working as a postdoc in sports psychology, a meditation course in the tradition of Zen Buddhism was offered.

With great enthusiasm, I attended the first session in the significantly overcrowded meditation room of the University of Konstanz and noticed after a short time that the long and upright sitting on the meditation bench was associated with numerous pains such as in the knee, back, or ankle. My body, marked by competitive sports, did not have the necessary flexibility to endure the sitting position for a long time. After a few minutes in the sitting position, my body resisted, so that concentration on the breath or anything else was hardly possible. Although the number of active course participants halved from week to week, I stubbornly stuck to my plan to learn the meditation techniques. I convinced myself that my body would sooner or later adapt to this sitting position and that I should just endure

## 3 The Mindfulness Program for Athletes          45

the exercise sessions. However, the inner resistance to regularly attend this course was always greater. After the eighth week, I too dropped out of the course. However, my ambition got the better of me, so I signed up for this meditation course again the next semester. This time I made it to the end of the semester and got to know all the exercises presented there.

In the next semester, I took up a junior professorship for sports psychology at the Humboldt University in Berlin, and there was a large offer of mindfulness and meditation courses. I signed up for several mindfulness courses, visited Buddhist meditation centers, and in this way soaked up the practical knowledge like a sponge. I tried out daily how which techniques work for me and separated the useful from the useless for sports. I understood that top and competitive athletes represent a special target group and that the usual mindfulness courses, such as MBSR or ACT, or religiously motivated practices would not work for them. The key to the successful implementation of mindfulness training in competitive sports lies in psychoeducation. Top and competitive athletes are a critical clientele who carefully weigh up the pros and cons before they even try out a new sports psychology program. Here, the arguments must be carefully and scientifically prepared and the exercises must be taken out of the spiritual or religious context.

During my time at the Humboldt University in Berlin, I got to know Christoph Kittler, who had just finished his studies in sports psychology and was looking for a PhD topic. I introduced him to the concept of mindfulness and he immediately understood the potential of mindfulness training for competitive sports. We both attended the Mindfulness-Based-Stress-Reduction(MBSR) course by Jon Kabat-Zin and discussed which exercises with which psychoeducation would make sense in the context of competitive sports. Christoph then went to New York for a semester and met George Mumford there, who had very successfully established mindfulness training with numerous athletes. After his return from the USA, we continued to work on the possible mindfulness program and we now created the first version of the Berlin Mindfulness Training in Competitive Sports (BATL) and tried it out with a top athlete.

The next step was to investigate the effectiveness of the newly developed mindfulness program. For this purpose, we recruited 46 sports science students and randomly assigned them to either the mindfulness group or a general sports psychology group. The aim of this first study was to investigate the effectiveness of the mindfulness intervention compared to traditional sports psychology training. In the course of this study, we showed that the participants in the mindfulness group had actually become more mindful

(Jekauc et al., 2016) and that their strategies for emotion regulation had changed positively compared to the control group (Kittler et al., 2018).

After this very productive time at the Humboldt University in Berlin, Christoph and I went our separate ways. I was offered a full professorship at the Goethe University Frankfurt am Main and then a regular professorship at the Karlsruhe Institute of Technology, which I accepted, while Christoph remained in Berlin as a practicing sports psychologist and advanced the topic as part of his doctoral thesis. While working with several athletes and through several courses, I noticed that the original form of the Berlin Mindfulness Training needed a few revisions. Step by step, I developed a successor program that had a lot in common with the Berlin Mindfulness Training in Competitive Sports in terms of the course concept, but differed significantly from it in the selection of exercises and psychoeducation. Finally, Lea Mülberger and Susanne Weyland shaped a version of the mindfulness training in sports that forms the basis of the program presented here.

## 3.4 Efficacy Verification

As explained in the previous section, Christoph Kittler focused on the effectiveness of Berlin mindfulness training in his doctoral thesis. A randomized study with sports science students showed that mindfulness training led to a significant increase in the personality trait of mindfulness (Jekauc et al., 2016) and a significant reduction in maladaptive emotion regulation strategies (Kittler et al., 2018). In another study with 137 elite adolescent athletes at a sports boarding school, it was further shown that Berlin mindfulness training led to significant increases in concentration performance (Kittler et al., 2022). Thus, the two most important mechanisms of mindfulness training were demonstrated, namely, that athletes in the context of competitive sports could improve concentration and emotion regulation.

In the clinical context, a number of studies show that mindfulness-based interventions have a positive impact on various aspects of physical and mental health (cf. Hölzel & Brähler, 2015). For example, a meta-analysis of 209 studies found that mindfulness-based interventions produced medium-sized effects in various mental disorders, comparable to traditional cognitive-behavioral interventions. Mindfulness training was particularly effective in treating anxiety symptoms and depression, where mindfulness interventions produced large effects. Even in non-clinical populations, one can expect medium to large effects on emotional constructs, relationship variables, and attention (Sedlmeier et al., 2012).

Furthermore, researchers have found, using neuroscientific methods such as electroencephalography or functional magnetic resonance imaging, how regular and systematic mindfulness meditation not only changes neural functions but also brain structures (see also Davidson et al., 2003). The studies suggest that mindfulness training promotes cognitive neuroplasticity (i.e., the ability to adapt neural structures) and improves the ability to regulate one's own emotions. Begley (2008) concludes that mindfulness training and meditative techniques shape the brain's emotional circuits as effectively as one can shape the muscles of the chest (2008). Overall, the conclusion can be drawn that mindfulness training works similarly to strength training. The abilities to maintain concentration and regulate one's own emotions can be trained like a muscle.

## 3.5 Course Structure

The APS Mindfulness Program for Athletes can be conducted in a group or alone. It includes eight course units, which are intended to lead to improved mindfulness and thus also to better performance in sports. All course units are similarly structured. The following section explains the individual components that make up all units, as well as the values that apply in the group throughout the entire mindfulness program. The eight course units are then presented.

The mindfulness program consists of a total of eight units of 90 min each, each unit containing special practical exercises such as breathing and meditation exercises. In addition to these exercises, processes are initiated within the program to learn more about oneself. This means not only reflecting on values, thought patterns, and routines, but also identifying stressors and eliminating them. The program is designed so that the exercises are initially practiced in a quiet environment and, as concentration and emotion regulation skills are increasingly acquired, are also applied in the sports context. Sport-specific psychological problems can be discussed in the group and solutions can be worked out at an individual level.

Different topics are covered in the different units. Firstly, an introduction to the topic of mindfulness takes place in the first unit. In the following seven units, topics are covered that can be influenced by mindfulness practices: self-awareness, everyday stress, body perceptions, the power of thoughts, the inner observer, emotions, and living in the here and now. The main form of stress here is cognitive performance, such as the ability to concentrate.

At the beginning of each unit, a minute of silence is observed to shed the stress of everyday life. This is followed by psychoeducation in the information phase, i.e., explanations are given on how the program works and what goals the respective exercises have. The texts provided for this can either be read out by a course leader or read independently. This is followed by practical exercises, which are then reflected on by the learners and, in the case of a course context, experiences are exchanged between the participants. Between the exercises, a story is read or read out, which is also reflected on by the learners. This serves to consolidate the content that has already been covered in the information phase. At the end of each course unit, the exercises for the coming week are planned and a final minute of silence is carried out. The individual components of the individual course units are explained in more detail below.

**Components of all Course Units**
1. **A Minute of Silence:**
   At the beginning of each course unit, a minute of silence takes place. Some learners or course participants arrive from a hectic everyday life and are not immediately ready to engage in mindfulness. The same can apply to individuals who are going through the program independently. The minute of silence is intended to lower the arousal level of the learners and create the conditions for the subsequent mindfulness exercises.
2. **Discussion of the Course Topic:**
   In the further course of each unit, the course topic is discussed in more detail. This is where psychoeducation takes place, where learners are informed about the background and effects of the exercises either by reading a text or through a lecture by a course leader. Athletes represent a very demanding clientele who want to be informed about the purpose and effects of the exercises. This is also intended to increase motivation to complete the program to the end.
3. **Practical Exercises:**
   Each course unit includes at least two practical exercises that promote mindfulness and the necessary auxiliary processes such as concentration. The length of the exercises increases over the course of the program, as learners are increasingly able to practice the exercises for longer periods. The first units start with a duration of three to four minutes per exercise, with the exercise duration increasing to up to 20 min by the end of the program. The exercises are ideally initiated and ended by a gong or a similar pleasant sound. Each practical exercise includes a reflection phase, in which learners either independently contemplate their meditation

experience or share their experiences with the group in a course context. To stimulate learners' reflection, possible reflection questions are provided for each exercise. The reflection phase is an important part of each mindfulness course unit, as this is often where learners' rethinking takes place. Therefore, it is important to allow sufficient time for this phase.

4. **Reflection and Discussion:**
Almost every course unit includes a story to promote reflection on one's own values and actions. Following this story, it is the learners' task to reflect on the contents of the story and, in the case of course participation, to share their thoughts about the story with the group. Since the learners are usually athletes, it is also possible to transfer aspects of the story to sports and, for example, share similar experiences from their everyday sports life with the rest of the group. It is important in reflecting on the story that there is no right or wrong interpretation. Questions that can contribute to stimulating the reflection or discussion round may include:

   – How would you interpret the story?
   – What stands out most to you from the story?
   – What do you think the story is trying to convey?
   – To which everyday situation can the story be applied?
   – To which sports situation can the story be applied?

   In addition to the learners' interpretations, possible interpretations are provided for each story, which can also be discussed or thought through after independent reflection.

5. **Planning of the Upcoming Practice Week:**
At the end of the program unit, the upcoming practice week is planned. The tasks mentioned here should not be seen as unwanted effort, as in school, but as the opportunity to consolidate valuable skills of mindfulness training already learned in the program and thus to continue to develop. Finally, a second minute of silence is carried out, which represents the end of the respective program unit.

6. **Exercise for Home:**
Homework is important for transferring mindfulness into practice. First, mindfulness should take hold in everyday life and then gradually be transferred to sports practice. Practicing mindfulness at home always consists of two components: A) practical application of meditation forms and B) creating the conditions for implementing mindfulness practice by reflecting on one's own thought patterns and values.

To record their own experiences and thoughts on the exercises, learners can use the diary page at the end of each course unit.

**Values in the Mindfulness Group**

If the program is conducted by a group, the following values should be communicated at the beginning of the course:

1. *Trust:* What happens and is said in the course, stays in the course.
2. *Punctuality:* Once the course has started, any entry or exit disrupts concentration.
3. *Keep calm:* There will certainly be one or another situation where the exercise does not work as desired. In this case, simply maintain calm until the end of the exercise.

# References

Begley, S. (2008). *Train your mind, change your brain: How a new science reveals our extraordinary potential to transform ourselves.* Ballantine Books.

Csikszentmihalyi, M. (1990). *Flow: The psychology of optimal experience.* Harper & Row.

Davidson, R. J., & Begley, S. (2012). *The emotional life of your brain: How its unique patterns affect the way you think, feel, and live—And how you can change them.* Hudson Street Press.

Davidson, R. J., Kabat-Zinn, J., Schumacher, J., Rosenkranz, M., Muller, D., Santorelli, S. F., … & Sheridan, J. F. (2003). Alterations in brain and immune function produced by mindfulness meditation. *Psychosomatic medicine, 65*(4), 564–570. https://doi.org/10.1097/01.PSY.0000077505.67574.E3.

Furley, P., & Schweizer, G. (2020). Body language in sport. In G. Tenenbaum & R. C. Eklund (Eds.), *Handbook of sport psychology* (4. edn., pp. 1201–1219). Wiley https://doi.org/10.1002/9781119568124.ch59.

Hölzel, B., & Brähler, C. (Eds.). (2015). *Achtsamkeit mitten im Leben. Anwendungsgebiete und wissenschaftliche Perspektiven.* OW Barth.

Jekauc, D., & Kittler, C. (2015). Achtsamkeit im Leistungssport. *Leistungssport, 45*(6), 19–23.

Jekauc, D., Kittler, C., & Schlagheck, M. (2016). Effectiveness of a mindfulness-based intervention for athletes. *Psychology, 8*(1), 1–13. https://doi.org/10.4236/psych.2017.81001.

Kittler, C., Gische, C., Arnold, M., & Jekauc, D. (2018). Der Einfluss eines achtsamkeitsbasierten Trainingsprogramms auf die Emotionsregulation von

Sportlerinnen und Sportlern. *Zeitschrift für Sportpsychologie, 25*(4), 146–155. https://doi.org/10.1026/1612-5010/a000242.

Kittler, C., Arnold, M., & Jekauc, D. (2022). Effects of a mindfulness-based intervention on sustained and selective attention in young top-level athletes in a school training setting: A randomized control trial study. *The Sport Psychologist, 1*(aop), 1–12. https://doi.org/10.1123/tsp.2021-0053.

Sedlmeier, P., Eberth, J., Schwarz, M., Zimmermann, D., Haarig, F., Jaeger, S., & Kunze, S. (2012). The psychological effects of meditation: A meta-analysis. *Psychological bulletin, 138*(6), 1139–1171. https://doi.org/10.1037/a0028168.

# 4

# Course Unit 1: Mindfulness—Arriving in the Here and Now

**Goals**

- Approaching the topic of mindfulness
- Improving concentration performance
- Conscious experience and acceptance of the current state

**Content: Introduction to the topic of mindfulness**
Mindfulness means consciously having attention in the present moment, without judging or evaluating it. The origin of mindfulness lies in a Buddhist way of thinking. A distinction is made between formal meditation, such as breath or walking meditation, and informal meditation, such as mindfulness in everyday life. The mechanisms of action of mindfulness training are: increased concentration ability, more frequent flow experiences, and improved emotion regulation ability.

**Procedure:**

- Minute of silence
- Greeting and mutual getting to know the course participants (in the case of a course context)
- Introduction to the topic of mindfulness
- Exercises: Breath meditation

  - Conscious abdominal breathing
  - Arm circling and breathing rhythm
  - Counting breaths

- Reflection on breath meditation
- Presentation of the mindfulness diary
- Planning for the upcoming practice week
- Minute of silence

© The Author(s), under exclusive license to Springer-Verlag GmbH, DE, part of Springer Nature 2024
D. Jekauc et al., *Mindfulness Training in Sport*,
https://doi.org/10.1007/978-3-662-68804-5_4

> **Preliminary exercise 1: Conscious abdominal breathing**
>
> - Inhalation: Bulging of the abdomen outwards
> - Exhalation: Movement of the abdomen inwards
>
> **Preliminary exercise 2: Arm circling and breathing rhythm**
>
> - Inhale: Stretch arms rather quickly from bottom to top
> - Exhale: Take arms rather slowly from the side of the body downwards
> - Let arm circling be controlled by the breathing rhythm
>
> **Exercise 1: Counting breaths (ABCD exercise)**
>
> - Inhale, exhale, 1
> - Inhale, exhale, 2
> - Count up to 10, then down to 1
>
> **Homework:**
>
> 1. Perform the breath meditation daily
> 2. Identification and reduction of distractions in everyday life

## Mindfulness—Arriving in the Here and Now
## A Minute of Silence

Each program unit begins with a minute of silence to arrive in the here and now.

## Introduction to the topic of mindfulness

Many have experienced this: You want to walk to a friend's house. The beginning of the route strongly resembles the way to work. Suddenly you find yourself—instead of in front of the friend's house—in front of your own workplace. You can't even remember whether you walked fast or slow, whether there was a lot or a little going on along the way, who you met on the way. How is it possible that you arrive at a place and are hardly aware of how you got there at all? This is possible when you are in autopilot mode. You have walked the route to work so often that it has become automated. Routines and habits per se are not bad. They allow you to focus your attention on other things. On the other hand, thought or action patterns can become habits that are not good for you. By acting in autopilot, actions and reactions from the past are repeatedly copied and you are hardly receptive to new options. If the autopilot takes over, the following behaviors can creep in:

## Example

| In the profession | In private life |
|---|---|
| Automated and routine task completion | Unconscious nutrition |
| Occurrence of errors | Inactivity and passivity |
| Lack of creativity | Caught in emotions and stress |
| Consolidation of thinking, feeling, and behavior patterns | |
| Stress | |

Highly automated movements also occur very frequently in sports. For example, most of an athlete's movements and actions consist of precise movement sequences, such as a tennis serve or a free kick in football, which have been trained over years. In this case, the trained automatisms of motor skills are very helpful in achieving top performance even under competitive conditions. Problems arise when emotional processes, such as competition anxiety, outbursts of anger, etc., are automated, which have a negative impact on performance. In such situations, one often acts hastily and drifts off in thought, playing through future scenarios, imagining the consequences of the outcome of the competition, or being annoyed about missed opportunities. In such highly emotional situations, one's thoughts are either in the future or in the past, missing the important moment.

The task of mindfulness training is to learn techniques to stay in the present and be there when it matters. It's about being mentally fully present and focused in important moments of the competition. Through this trained permanent focus on what is happening right now, we learn step by step to become more relaxed and to deal more relaxedly with our own mistakes and mishaps in competition. This transformation from a fearful, emotional, or even headless player to an emotionally stable and focused athlete is a long way and requires a lot of training. As we have seen in the theory part of this book using the case of Djokovic, mindfulness training can be compared to physical training, which must be practiced daily to achieve visible success.

In order to successfully implement mindfulness training in everyday life, certain mental and temporal resources are necessary. Conditions must be created under which mindfulness can develop. Mindfulness cannot develop if we are stressed all day or constantly exposed to other stimuli. Therefore, the first step is to reduce the distractions, such as a flood of emails, messages from social networks, background noise from television, etc. It is necessary to critically examine and possibly change one's own habits in dealing with the flood of information. Periods of rest must be created so that mindfulness has a chance to develop at all.

The term mindfulness means consciously perceiving what is happening right now, without evaluating. Specifically, mindfulness can be understood as a mental skill that consists of two components.

*Firstly*, it is about building and maintaining *mental presence* over a certain period of time. This mental presence requires cognitive resources, such as attention and concentration. So, one can only be present in the moment if one has a certain ability to concentrate and can maintain this concentration over a certain period of time. Therefore, a considerable part of mindfulness training also aims at improving the ability to concentrate. Our brain is designed in such a way that it constantly generates new thoughts, which are associatively linked to each other and appear in the form of chains of thoughts. It is estimated that about 80,000 thoughts go through our heads every day. Mindfulness also means noticing what is going through our heads and becoming the guide of these thoughts. Many of these thoughts repeat themselves over and over again and do not get us anywhere. One goal of mindfulness training is to free oneself from these thoughts and to notice what is happening in this moment. But it is also about identifying and gradually eliminating the distractions in our life that trigger these thoughts and feelings. This is how we create the conditions to cultivate mindfulness in our life.

*Secondly*, mindfulness also involves adopting a *non-judgmental attitude* and accepting things as they are. When we evaluate how the situation is, how we and others are, it brings a certain emotionality that makes life difficult for us in many situations. The ability to accept things as they are gives us a certain emotional stability and helps us to go through the day more calmly. The mental attitude cannot simply be decided, but must be practiced day by day to become our attitude towards life. As part of mindfulness training, exercises are practiced weekly that aim to create space for the development of this mental attitude.

Meditations are a way to implement mindfulness in life and understand thoughts. A basic distinction is made between formal and informal meditation. Exercises, as described in the following in this book, such as breath or walking meditation, are considered formal meditations. Mindful action in everyday life, on the other hand, is considered informal meditation techniques.

The effect of mindfulness practices has now been scientifically demonstrated in several areas. This is also a reason for the image change of mindfulness. In sports psychology, three mechanisms are suspected for the positive effects on athletic performance (Jekauc & Kittler, 2015). These three mechanisms of action are based on promoting concentration, training emotion regulation, and experiencing flow (Fig. 4.1). Concentration is a prerequisite for top performance in many sports. Since mindfulness training promotes concentration, performance will also benefit from it. Positive emotions in sports can also enhance performance. While negative emotions, for example in the form of competition anxiety, have negative effects on performance by narrowing the focus of attention and inhibiting the efficiency of cognitive information processing, positive emotions have an opposite, performance-enhancing effect. Through mindfulness practices, negative emotions can be pushed into the background and positive emotions can be promoted, thereby positively influencing performance. Finally, flow states are also said to improve an athlete's performance. This flow experience is understood as a balance between the challenges and the existing abilities and thus as a state of optimal performance. When you experience a flow moment, negative thoughts and self-doubts recede into the background and this creates space for positive feelings. The effect of mindfulness training can be that the occurrence of flow experiences is promoted and their level can be increased, leading to an improvement in performance.

There are therefore many ways in which mindfulness-based training positively influences both our everyday life and specifically the performance of

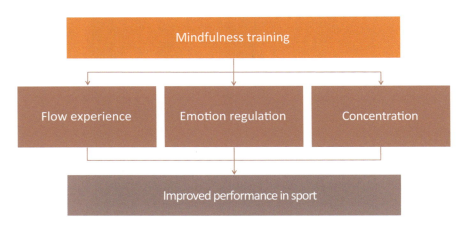

**Fig. 4.1** Mechanisms of action of mindfulness training

athletes. The exercises of the mindfulness program lay the first foundation for anchoring more mindfulness in life and thinking.

**Practical exercises and reflection: Breathing meditations**
**Preliminary exercise 1: Conscious abdominal breathing**

**Background information**
Starting position: Comfortable and stable sitting position
Duration: 5 min
Benefit: Activation of the diaphragm

**Instructions for execution**
Get into a comfortable yet stable sitting position (Figs. 4.2 and 4.3), where you have enough room to breathe. You can rest your hands loosely on your lap. If you like, close your eyes. Now focus on abdominal breathing. Let the

**Fig. 4.2** Sitting position (side view)

**Fig. 4.3** Sitting position (front view)

breath arrive in the abdomen, not in the chest or shoulders. Do you feel the rise and fall of the abdominal wall when breathing? For better perception, you can gently place your hands on your abdominal wall. Now breathe very consciously into your hands and then let all the air out again. Let the breath flow as it does on its own.

> **Reflection**
> Afterwards, the learners reflect on their meditation experience. If the mindfulness program is carried out in a course with several participants, the participants can share their experiences of the exercise with the group. Participants are often reassured when they hear that everyone finds it difficult to concentrate at first.
> The learners' reflection can be stimulated by the following questions:
>
> - How did you perceive your breath? Where did you feel it?
> - Did you find it difficult to breathe into your abdomen?
> - Does abdominal breathing feel different than your everyday breathing?

## Preliminary exercise 2: Arm circling and breathing rhythm

**Background information**
Starting position: Standing with legs spread shoulder-width apart
Duration: 3–4 min
Benefit: Finding rhythm and conscious control of relaxation and tension as well as deceleration of the exhalation process

**Instructions for Execution**
Stand upright, circle your shoulders a few times loosely backwards and then lower them down at the back. Now focus on your breath. As you inhale, swing your arms up in front of your body in a rather quick movement. As you exhale, take your arms down to the sides of your body and take your time with this movement. Breathe in dynamically and take your arms over your head and let your arms slowly come down to the side as you exhale. Find a rhythm that feels natural and perform the arm circles several times. Fig. 4.4 illustrates the process of arm circling.

> **Reflection**
> The learners' reflection can be stimulated by the following questions:
>
> - How did you perceive your breath? Where did you feel it?
> - Were you able to find a pleasant, natural rhythm?

**Fig. 4.4** Arm Circling

## 4 Course Unit 1: Mindfulness—Arriving in the Here and Now 61

### Exercise 1: Counting Breath (ABCD Exercise)

**Background Information**
Starting position: Comfortable and stable sitting position
Duration: 7 min
Benefits: Conscious experience of the present moment and acceptance of the current state, focus on breathing

| | |
|---|---|
| A = Upright posture | B = Abdominal breathing |
| C = Counting | D = Thinking |

### Instructions for Execution

Sit upright on the chair. The feet are flat on the floor. Rest your hands on your thighs. Notice the contact with the floor and the chair. Make a few circular movements with your shoulders, pull your shoulders up to your ears and let them sink down at the back as you exhale. Now you can let your shoulders hang relaxed, supported by the hands on your thighs. Relax your facial muscles and close your eyes. Try to maintain a pleasant level of tension in the back muscles, do not become too slack and slump, but also do not tense up too hard.

Now focus on the *abdominal breathing*. Let the breath arrive in the abdomen, not in the chest or shoulders. Do you feel the rise and fall of the abdominal wall as you breathe? Let the breath flow as it does on its own. The breath is the anchor of attention. You can always return to it when your thoughts wander. Try to observe the events as neutrally and openly as possible, without judgment and evaluation, as if you were watching small waves on the shore of a river. You can also place your hands on your abdomen to feel the breath even better.

Now start with the third part, the *counting*. Count each breath as follows: Inhale, exhale, 1, inhale, exhale, 2, etc. Count in this way breath by breath up to 10 and then backwards breath by breath: Inhale, exhale, 9, inhale, exhale, 8 etc. When you get back to 1, count the breaths again ascending to 10, then go backwards again.

Now come to the *thinking*. It happens again and again that thoughts come up during the exercise that distract you. This is normal and no reason to get upset. If you notice that your attention has wandered with your thoughts, gently bring it back to the observation of the breath. Focus your attention again completely on the rise and fall of your abdominal wall and count the next breaths—just start again at 1 if you are unsure where you had stopped. Try it now without guidance for a few minutes. Remember the ABCD, an upright posture, attention on abdominal breathing and counting the breaths, to which you can always return when thoughts distract you.

And now slowly direct your attention back to your surroundings, pay attention to the sounds in the room that surrounds you. Feel the air on your skin and the light shimmering through your eyelids. And when you are ready, gently open your eyes again and fully return to the outside world.

> **Reflection**
>
> The reflection of the learners can be stimulated by the following questions:
>
> - How did you perceive your breath? Where did you feel it?
> - How well were you able to keep your concentration on your breathing?
> - Did many thoughts go through your head?
> - If you drifted away from your breath, what kind of thoughts came up in you?
> - Were you able to return to your breath after you drifted away?

## Planning the upcoming practice week

Implementing mindfulness into one's daily life is a long process. Only through sufficient practice can mindfulness have positive effects on behavior and perception. Therefore, it is useful to collect one's experiences in practicing mindfulness during the duration of this program and to record these in a mindfulness diary.

It is advantageous for the learners' motivation, among other things, to note practice times, duration of practice, and type of meditation. This way, they can become aware of their progress through the frequency of execution.

In addition to the hard facts about their meditation style, learners can also record their perceptions during meditation in a diary. The diary page prepared for each program unit at the end of the respective section can be used for this purpose. The following questions can be helpful for reflection and the thoughts on this can be noted in the diary:

- What physical sensations did I experience?
- What thoughts went through my head?
- Did something distract me? What was it?

Absolute honesty is necessary when keeping a mindfulness diary. There is no right or wrong. The mindfulness diary is only useful if one is completely

## 4 Course Unit 1: Mindfulness—Arriving in the Here and Now 63

honest with oneself and records the actual progress, but perhaps also setbacks, truthfully for oneself in order to be able to learn from it.

Mindfulness needs space to be cultivated. A packed daily routine and constant background stimuli make it difficult to lead a mindful life. Therefore, part of a mindful life is to reconsider one's own activities and decide what is important to one and what one can do without in life. In doing so, one will certainly come across background activities that have crept unnoticed into our lives. This could be, for example, constantly checking the phone for new messages. The first practice week also involves recognizing such habits and eliminating the distractions from one's own life.

Since the practice of mindfulness practices is absolutely necessary for the implementation of mindfulness in everyday life, homework is given to the learners every week in connection with the respective course content, which they should carry out daily until the next course unit and record their experiences. The homework always consists of the two areas *Practical practice of mindfulness* and *Observation and restructuring of everyday life*.

The following two tasks support the first entry into lived mindfulness:

1. Perform a daily breath meditation in a quiet environment for 5–7 min. Try to practice the exercise at the same time if possible.
2. Ask yourself daily what external distractions occur in your everyday life and how they can be reduced. This could mean, for example, that you refrain from listening to the radio on the next car ride and concentrate exclusively on the road, or drink the next breakfast coffee without reading the newspaper at the same time.

## Minute of Silence

| | Disruptive stimuli in everyday life (e.g. radio on the car journey, ...) | Meditation exercise |
|---|---|---|
| Monday | | |
| Tuesday | | |
| Wednesday | | |
| Thursday | | |
| Friday | | |
| Saturday | | |
| Sunday | | |

# References

Jekauc, D., & Kittler, C. (2015). Achtsamkeit im Leistungssport. *Leistungssport, 45*(6), 19–23.

# 5

# Course Unit 2: Mindfulness as a Means of Self-Realization

**Goals**

- Consolidation and expansion of the learned meditation (breath meditation)
- Transfer of mindfulness practice into everyday life
- Self-realization

**Content: Autopilot**
Automated thought patterns help to classify situations more quickly. Nevertheless, it is important to regularly reflect on existing thought patterns (as well as values and attitudes) and to check whether they fit the current stage of life.

**Procedure:**

- Minute of silence
- Recapitulation of the last practice week
- Psychoeducation
- Exercise 1: Counting breaths
- Reflection of Exercise 1
- Exercise 2: Walking meditation
- Reflection of Exercise 2
- Exercise 3: Creation of a life tree
- Planning of the upcoming practice week
- Minute of silence

**Exercise 1: Counting breaths (ABCD exercise)**

- Inhale, exhale, 1
- Inhale, exhale, 2
- Count up to 10, then down to 1

© The Author(s), under exclusive license to Springer-Verlag GmbH, DE, part of Springer Nature 2024
D. Jekauc et al., *Mindfulness Training in Sport*,
https://doi.org/10.1007/978-3-662-68804-5_5

66        D. Jekauc et al.

**Exercise 2: Walking meditation**

- Participants move
- Slow walking in a circle
- Steps are in rhythm with the breath

**Exercise 3: Life tree**

- Drawing of a tree
- Trunk: the four most important values
- Branches: important areas of life
- Leaves: joyful activities related to the respective branches
- Decision for shallow or deep root system

**Homework:**

1. Perform one of the two exercises once a day.
2. Determine everyday actions that you want to design mindfully from now on.
3. Finalize your life tree.

## Mindfulness as a means of self-realization

### A minute of silence

Each course unit begins with a minute of silence to arrive in the here and now. After the minute of silence, what was practiced in the previous week is recapitulated independently or in a group context. The learners reflect on their weekly progress and tell about good, but also worse experiences.

### The Autopilot

Athletes and coaches often only come to a psychologist when a serious problem has already arisen. It is much more advisable to build a foundation of mindfulness that already exists in times of crisis, rather than starting to intervene in times of crisis. The previous course unit described the importance of the autopilot for athletes: how it facilitates some things, e.g. the serve in tennis or a shot in football, but also complicates some things, e.g. competition anxiety and outbursts of anger. In order to change this autopilot and adapt it to one's own benefit, one must first become aware of how it is programmed.

As a rule, the autopilot is based on one's own ideas, habits that one has trained over many years, and also on experiences that one has gone through. Values that one adopts from parents or friends can reinforce a rigid pattern

## 5 Course Unit 2: Mindfulness as a Means of Self-Realization 67

of thinking and acting in the autopilot. The thoughts generated by the autopilot facilitate orientation in the world and also make it easier to understand new situations, as the new is compared with the known and reactions can be generalized accordingly. The thought patterns that arise from this can be imagined like a walk through the forest. If you take a path for the first time, there are branches and stones in the way, the ground is uneven and you have to concentrate hard not to stumble. However, if you take this path over and over again, a small beaten path is created. The more often you take this exact path, the better and faster you can manage the path.

In the case that one gets used to things that are not helpful, such as negative thoughts that reduce performance, one must find the right turn in this image of the walk in the forest and take new paths. However, before this is possible, one must first look at what is going on inside oneself. Often one does not notice all this anymore due to the fast-paced and stressful everyday life. Mindfulness is a way to change exactly that. You can take a step back and thus look more differentiated at what is going on inside you and analyze yourself. The view of oneself, one's thoughts and habits is only possible when one is calm.

**The right time—the calm lake**
Our inner self can be imagined like a lake. It is deep and many emotional and cognitive processes take place below the surface, which cannot be directly observed. As a rule, from the outside you only see what is happening on the surface, e.g. behavior, emotional expression, verbal communication, and this is actually only the expression of what is happening inside. To understand oneself, the lake must be clear and calm so that one can see to the bottom of the lake. In the phases of life when it gets stormy, waves appear on the surface of the lake and you cannot see the bottom. The same applies to our inner self during a stressful phase, in which one does not take the time to calm down. However, this is necessary to be able to see the bottom of the lake, i.e. our thoughts and experiences.

The year of an athlete runs in so-called cycles. Depending on the sport, the year is divided into one, two or even three cycles. Such a cycle begins with a training phase in which the conditional and technical prerequisites for the subsequent performance phases are created. The second phase involves a gradual transition to the competition phase. The third phase can be described as the high-performance phase, in which the most important competitions take place. From a psychological point of view, this is the most demanding phase in which many mental resources are used up. Finally, there is a relatively short regeneration phase in which one deals with the past cycle and gathers strength for the coming cycle. When implementing mindfulness training, one must carefully choose the timing. The regeneration phase or the training phase represent the ideal time when one should start training mindfulness.

Let's take the example of tennis. The tournaments where everyone who values themselves wants to be in top form are Roland Garros and Wimbledon between May and July. This would be the worst possible time to start mindfulness training. Instead, one should wait until this stormy phase is over and one is in the regeneration or training phase. Only in these quiet phases does the athlete get enough rest to identify and eliminate disturbances. During this time, one can ask oneself the questions: "What is good for me?", "In what environment do I feel comfortable?" or "What stresses me and why?". In addition, during this time, one can reconsider value concepts that one has gained thoughtlessly. They are there, but have never been reflected upon. To address such fundamental questions, the lake must be calm and the water clear. The process of getting to know oneself and changing thought patterns and values is a long-term process that lasts a lifetime. With mindfulness techniques, one can trigger something in oneself, through which one perceives oneself more, constantly looks at oneself from the outside and analyzes and adjusts one's actions and thinking.

## Mindfulness as a means of self-knowledge

A first important step towards self-knowledge is the recognition of one's own values. Values serve as fixed stars in our lives, giving us orientation. They determine what is important to us and what we consider right or wrong. A violation of one's own values usually leads to a strong emotional reaction. An athlete, for example, for whom fair play is an important value, will react emotionally in situations when other athletes allow even minor rule violations. Another athlete may hardly react emotionally in comparable situations because fair play is not very important to her or she has a different understanding of fair play. Values vary from culture to culture, from individual to individual. The problem with recognizing one's own values and beliefs is that they are not always conscious and often direct our lives from the background. Perhaps we were told in childhood that we were too bad, too fat or too weak. Or we always had to be friendly and obedient, believe in a god or become rich someday. As adults, however, we have forgotten to critically review such evaluations. It would give us a lot of clarity if we really consciously noticed what we are convinced of and what we have uncritically adopted from others.

## 5 Course Unit 2: Mindfulness as a Means of Self-Realization        69

### Practical exercises and reflection

### Exercise 1: Counting breaths (ABCD exercise)

**Background information**
Starting position: Comfortable and stable sitting position
Duration: 8 min
Benefits: Conscious experience of the present moment and acceptance of the current state, focus on breathing

| | |
|---|---|
| A = Upright posture | B = Belly breathing |
| C = Counting | D = Thinking |

### Instructions for execution
Sit upright on the chair. Your feet are flat on the floor. Rest your hands on your thighs. Feel the contact with the floor and the chair. Make a few circular movements with your shoulders, pull your shoulders up to your ears and let them sink back down while exhaling. Now you can let your shoulders hang relaxed, supported by the hands on your thighs. Relax your facial muscles and close your eyes. Try to maintain a pleasant level of tension in the back muscles, not to become too slack and slump, but also not to tense up too hard.

Now focus on *belly breathing*. Let the breath arrive in the belly, not in the chest or shoulders. Do you feel the rise and fall of the abdominal wall when breathing? Let the breath flow as it does on its own. The breath is the anchor of attention. You can always return to it when your thoughts wander. Try to observe the events as neutrally and openly as possible, without judgment and evaluation, as if you were watching small waves on the shore of a river. You can also place your hands on your abdomen to feel the breath even better.

Now start with the third part, the *counting*. Count each breath as follows: Inhale, exhale, 1, inhale, exhale, 2, etc. Count in this way breath for breath up to 10 and then backwards breath for breath: Inhale, exhale, 9, inhale, exhale, 8, etc. When you are back at 1, count the breaths again ascending to 10, then it goes backwards again.

Now come to *thinking*. It happens again and again that thoughts come up during the exercise that distract you. This is normal and no reason to get upset. If you notice that your attention has gone for a walk with your thoughts, gently bring it back to breath observation. Focus your attention again completely on the rise and fall of your abdominal wall and count the next breaths - just start again at 1 if you are unsure where you left off. Try it now without guidance for a few minutes. Think of the ABCD, an upright posture, attention on belly breathing and counting the breaths, to which you can always return when thoughts distract you.

And now slowly direct your attention back to your surroundings, pay attention to the sounds in the room that surrounds you. Feel the air on your skin and the light shimmering through your eyelids. And when you are ready, gently open your eyes again and fully return to the outside world.

> **Reflection**
>
> The learners' reflection can be stimulated by the following questions:
>
> - How did you perceive your breath? Where did you feel it?
> - How well were you able to stay with your concentration on your breathing?
> - Did many thoughts go through your head?
> - When you drifted away from your breath, what kind of thoughts came up in you?
> - How well were you able to return to your breath after you had drifted away?

## Exercise 2: Walking meditation

### Background information
Starting position: Free standing in the room
Duration: 8 min
Benefits: Training of conscious perception and concentration

### Instructions for Execution
Stand up and breathe in and out several times. Once you have calmed down and your breath has settled, become aware of it. Feel the rhythm of your breath and start walking slowly. Breathe in and take a step forward. The foot with which you step forward is placed on the heel during inhalation, so that the body weight is still on the back leg. Breathe out and now place the entire foot on the ground, so that the body weight shifts forward during exhalation. On the next inhalation, you place the other foot forward on the heel, on exhalation you again shift the body weight and place the entire foot on the ground. The Fig. 5.1 illustrates the walking meditation. Make sure that your pace does not dictate your breathing rhythm, but that breathing initiates the movement. Try to be present with your breath, accept other participants or noises as they are, without them influencing your breathing

**Fig. 5.1** Walking Meditation

and movement. If your thoughts wander, accept that too and return to your breath. If your breathing rhythm changes, so does your pace.

Now slowly come to a standstill, breathe in and out deeply a few more times and direct your attention back to your surroundings.

> **Reflection**
>
> The learners' reflection can be stimulated by the following questions:
>
> - Were you able to focus well on your breathing rhythm?
> - Did you quickly find your walking pace?
> - Did you still let your walking pace be determined by your breathing rhythm after a while and not the other way around?
> - Did you notice other people or noises?

## Exercise 3: Tree of Life

### Background Information
Duration: 30 min
Benefit: Reflection of personal values

### Instructions for Implementation
For the Tree of Life exercise, a blank sheet and pens are necessary.

The Tree of Life exercise serves to reflect on one's own life and values. With this exercise, one should find out what really moves them and what is important to them. Many of our values are partly unconscious, and with this exercise, these values can be identified and visually represented. By becoming aware of one's own values, these can be critically reflected upon and possibly changed. Because our values, whether they act consciously or unconsciously, guide our actions and influence our feelings and moods. If we know our values, we will also understand ourselves and our emotions.

Gradually, you will fill the blank sheet in front of you with your Tree of Life. Start by drawing the trunk of the tree. This trunk should symbolize the foundation of your life. Consider which four values are most important to you in your life, so important that it would feel strange to live a day not according to these values. Write these four values into the trunk of your Tree of Life. After each word you have written down, consider what it actually means and whether it really says exactly what you mean. Be very honest with yourself. It's not about the values that others would expect from you, but about those that are really important to you. Maybe you write loyalty, but you actually mean above all that others should be loyal to you, and so you might realize that it's actually more about the value of appreciation. If you notice that you have written a word that doesn't exactly fit you, just correct yourself and in the end, really only write down the four values that make up your foundation.

Building on the trunk, you next draw branches. Each branch should correspond to an area of life that you find important. From each branch, draw fine offshoots to which you can write the values that are particularly important to you in relation to the corresponding area of life. Feel free to choose a few more than four, you can write up to ten values for each branch.

Finally, leaves should grow from the branches. Write the activities next to these leaves that you particularly enjoy in the corresponding area of life. If a leaf grows from the branch that is supposed to represent the area of life work, you could write something like lunch break with colleagues, reading, appointment for after-work beer, or similar—just all the topics that are related to the branch and enrich this area of life for you.

Your Tree of Life is almost finished. But what has the trunk actually grown from? What roots support it? Draw the roots under your tree that correspond to how rooted you feel. If you need routines and are a creature of habit, then your roots might be thick and reach deep into the ground, so that no one can easily transplant the tree. But if you are already planning your next move in your mind and are rather a flexible person, then the roots will be thin, so that the tree could be dug up.

## 5 Course Unit 2: Mindfulness as a Means of Self-Realization 73

When you look at your finished Tree of Life, you can imagine where it actually grows. What does the environment look like, is it a tree that loves swamps, thrives by the lake, or prefers dry soil and lots of sun? Consider whether the tree stands in a forest full of other trees or off to the side, rather alone. And last but not least: What does the tree actually radiate?

> **Reflection**
> Creating a Tree of Life is a very personal experience. Participants should therefore have the choice to share this reflection with the group or to keep it to themselves.

### Planning the Upcoming Exercise Week
1. Perform one of the two exercises (counting breaths or walking meditation) once a day. Commit to one of the two exercises at the beginning of the week so that it can be practiced intensively.
2. Choose an everyday action, e.g. the morning coffee, which you want to perform mindfully from now on. Set a fixed time of the day for this action to make it a habit.

Since the time frame in the case of a course taking place often does not suffice to create a Tree of Life, participants are additionally asked to complete their Tree of Life at home.

3. Finalize the Tree of Life that you have already started in the course unit.

## Minute of Silence

| | Mindful everyday actions (e.g. drinking coffee, brushing teeth, ...) | Meditation exercise |
|---|---|---|
| Monday | | |
| Tuesday | | |
| Wednesday | | |
| Thursday | | |
| Friday | | |
| Saturday | | |
| Sunday | | |

# 6

# Course Unit 3: Deepening the Topic of Breath Meditation

**Goals**

- Identification of stressors in everyday life
- Promoting focus on the breath

**Content: Mindfulness—a tool against stress**
Stress is a constant companion in a time when efficiency and productivity are becoming increasingly important. What many do not know: Multitasking does not save time. In fact, it is significantly more efficient (and makes you happier) if you only focus on the task at hand. This also applies to athletes, in whose lives stress is a fixed component due to the many competitions. Therefore, it is particularly important for them to confront emerging stress with emotional strength and focus on the here and now.

**Procedure:**

- Minute of silence
- Recapitulation of the last practice week
- Psychoeducation
- Exercise 1: Counting breaths
- Reflection of the First practical exercise
- Story "The Man and the Leopard"
- Exercise 2: Observing the breath
- Reflection of the Second practical exercise
- Planning of the upcoming practice week
- Minute of silence

© The Author(s), under exclusive license to Springer-Verlag GmbH, DE, part of Springer Nature 2024
D. Jekauc et al., *Mindfulness Training in Sport*,
https://doi.org/10.1007/978-3-662-68804-5_6

## Exercise 1: Counting breaths (ABCD exercise)

- Inhale, exhale, 1
- Inhale, exhale, 2
- Count up to 10, then down to 1

## Exercise 2: Observing the breath

- Close eyes and feel into the body
- Focus on breath and use it to stay present with attention.
- Observe breath without directly influencing it and find own rhythm
- Accept mental drifting and return to breath
- To end the exercise, slowly direct attention back to the surroundings and open the eyes.

## Homework:

1. Perform one of the two exercises once a day.
2. Identify and note down stressful situations in your everyday life.

## Deepening the topic of breath meditation

### A Minute of Silence

Each course unit begins with a minute of silence to arrive in the here and now.

### Mindfulness—a remedy against stress

One thing will be the same for most people: They practice multitasking. You make a phone call, see that an email has arrived in your inbox and quickly answer it—after all, this saves time, right? No, it actually doesn't. The hope of increasing productivity through multitasking is a misconception. Instead, you overwhelm yourself and create stress. A study (Killingsworth & Gilbert, 2010) asked people what they were working on at that moment and what they were thinking about at the same time. Those whose concentration and thus thoughts were focused on what they were doing at the moment were happier than those where there was a discrepancy between action and thought. This means that we feel better when we are fully engaged in what we are doing.

But what generally constitutes a stressful situation? Stress is always something emotional. It doesn't necessarily have to be negative, but stress often arises when a situation is significant to oneself and one fears not being able to cope with it. Therefore, it is important to know one's own limits and values and to know what is important to oneself. Because only when one is

## 6 Course Unit 3: Deepening the Topic of Breath Meditation

aware of this can one understand which situations appear stressful. This is also underscored by the fact that stress is always something subjective and never something objective. Stress is not caused by external factors, instead, we allow the stress to arise within ourselves.

All of this also applies to athletes. In sports, stress is primarily caused by pressure and the expectations that one imposes on oneself or that are imposed by one's environment. It is in the nature of things that an athlete is stressed before a competition, after all, competitions are important to athletes and they are emotionally involved. If a competition meant nothing to an athlete, they would also be indifferent to the outcome of the event, and no excitement or stress would arise.

So, this stress cannot really be switched off. Instead, one can change how one deals with the stress. One way to change the relationship with stress is to always be in the here and now. This means that when executing a behavior, one should be fully concentrated.

As an athlete, one is constantly compared to other athletes. Sometimes one has to prove oneself in front of the coaching team and other times in front of the fans. This constant comparison creates stress, which is part of competitive sports. The problem is that one internalizes the comparisons and no longer consciously perceives them. Comparisons are made constantly. However, if these comparisons are generalized to other areas of life, then stress can get out of hand and become unbearable. Performance comparisons in competition are part of an athlete's life, but the constant comparisons outside of competitions weigh heavily on the mood and feel like a backpack. Through mindfulness training, one becomes more sensitive to the everyday comparisons that make life difficult. One learns which comparisons are actually useful and how to distance oneself from these comparisons.

**Practical Exercises and Reflection**
**Exercise 1: Counting Breath (ABCD Exercise)**

**Background Information**
Starting position: Comfortable and stable sitting position
Duration: 10 min
Benefit: Training of concentration and preparation for more complex forms of meditation

| | |
|---|---|
| A = Upright posture | B = Belly breathing |
| C = Counting | D = Thinking |

## Instructions for Execution

Sit upright on the chair. Your feet are flat on the floor. Rest your hands on your thighs. Feel the contact with the floor and the chair. Make a few circular movements with your shoulders, then pull your shoulders up to your ears and let them sink back down while exhaling. Now you can let your shoulders hang relaxed, supported by your hands on your thighs. Relax your facial muscles and close your eyes. Try to maintain a pleasant level of tension in your back muscles, not to become too slack and slump, but also not to tense up too much.

Now focus on *abdominal breathing*. Let the breath arrive in your stomach, not in your chest or shoulders. Do you feel the rise and fall of your abdominal wall when breathing? Let the breath flow as it does on its own. The breath is the anchor of attention. You can always return to it when your thoughts wander. Try to observe the events as neutrally and openly as possible, without judgment and evaluation, as if you were watching small waves on the shore of a river. You can also place your hands on your abdominal wall to feel the breath even better.

Now start with the third part, the *counting*. Count each breath as follows: Inhale, exhale, 1, inhale, exhale, 2, etc. Count in this way breath by breath up to 10 and then backwards breath by breath: inhale, exhale, 9, inhale, exhale, 8, etc. When you are back at 1, count the breaths again ascending to 10, then it goes backwards again.

Now move on to *thinking*. It happens again and again that thoughts come up during the exercise that distract you. This is normal and no reason to get upset. If you notice that your attention has wandered with your thoughts, gently bring it back to observing your breath. Focus your attention again completely on the rise and fall of your abdominal wall and count the next breaths - just start again at 1 if you are unsure where you left off. Try it now without guidance for a few minutes. Think of the ABCD, an upright posture, attention on abdominal breathing and counting the breaths, to which you can always return when thoughts distract you.

And now slowly direct your attention back to your surroundings, pay attention to the sounds in the room that surrounds you. Feel the air on your skin and the light shimmering through your eyelids. And when you are ready, gently open your eyes again and now fully return to the outside world.

## 6 Course Unit 3: Deepening the Topic of Breath Meditation

**Reflection**

The learners' reflection can be stimulated by the following questions:

- How did you perceive your breath? Where did you feel it?
- How well were you able to stay focused on your breathing?
- Did many thoughts go through your head?
- When you drifted away from your breath, what kind of thoughts came up in you?
- Were you able to return to your breath after you had drifted away?

## Story for Reflection: The Man and the Leopard

"A man was on his way back to his village. He walked across the harvested rice fields on a wide plain along the edge of the forest. When a leopard came out of the forest, he saw that this leopard was hunting. He had the look that cats have when they are hungry. The man was greatly frightened, for there was no protection far and wide. The only thing he saw was a wooden stick lying near him. He kept a close eye on the leopard. The animal also kept looking at him with its hunting cat gaze and approached him. The man grabbed the stick and held it firmly in his hand. The stick was his only chance to defend his life against the leopard. The leopard hesitated whether to attack or retreat, for he sensed the man's determination to defend himself. The animal did not approach any further, but ran parallel to the man, who continued towards the village. The man held the stick tightly, kept an eye on the leopard and stayed as calm as he could, willing to defend his life. Finally, the man reached the village boundary, and the leopard disappeared back into the forest. The man threw away the stick. It broke into a thousand pieces. It was rotten." (quoted from Späth & Bao, 2011, p. 46). *quote translated from German*

## Discussion

The story is intended to encourage learners to form their views on what they have read/heard and to find possibilities for transfer to sports. In addition to the learners' interpretations, the following approaches can also be discussed (in the group):

- The stick gave the man the necessary self-confidence to believe that he would come out of this stressful situation unscathed.
- The man embodied determination. By radiating this or other emotions, you have a lot of influence on what others think of you and how they deal with you accordingly.

- The strength of the man in the story is his convincing body language. What role does body language play in your sport? What would you like to radiate?

### Exercise 2: Observing Breathing

**Background Information**
Starting position: Comfortable and stable sitting position
Duration: 10 min
Benefit: Training of conscious perception and concentration

### Instructions for Implementation
In this meditation, the attention should be directed to the breath. First, you should find a sitting position in which you can sit comfortably for a long time without having to move back and forth. To calm thoughts and feelings, it can be helpful to first bring the body to rest. So find a posture that is comfortable and stable and allows you to keep your back straight. Not rigid or cramped, but so that you can breathe easily and naturally into your stomach and all parts of the body can be well supplied with blood. Now slowly close your eyes and bring your attention to the present, to the here and now. Find out what there is to discover here. Feel what your body feels like, are there certain sensations or pains? And where is your body relaxed? Pay attention to the sounds around you. And what feelings are moving you inside? Fear or tension, hope, affection? And which thoughts push themselves into the foreground? All this belongs to you and your life: sensations, feelings, thoughts. And now, in the midst of all this, become aware of the fact that you are breathing. Or in other words: that breathing is happening. We want to use the movement of the breath to practice staying in the present with our attention. How do you perceive the breath? A coolness in the back of the throat when inhaling? The warmth of the exhaled air, a tingling? The movement of your chest, the stomach that rises and falls?

Feel your breath, but try not to change or control it. Just become aware of it, and let it find its own rhythm. Your body breathes by itself. For the

# 6 Course Unit 3: Deepening the Topic of Breath Meditation    81

next ten minutes, just feel each breath as it flows in and out. No matter where it makes itself noticeable, in the nose, in the throat, in the stomach. Feel each breath completely. You will notice that your thoughts wander. Plans or memories distract you. Don't get upset about it! Each time you become aware of it, look at these thoughts from the outside. Let them go again. Return to your breath. Imagine how the breath brings oxygen into your body, which is absorbed into the blood in the lungs, and is distributed throughout your body with each beat of your heart.

And now slowly turn your attention back to your surroundings, pay attention to the sounds in the room that surrounds you. Feel the air on your skin and the light that shimmers through your eyelids. And when you are ready, gently open your eyes again, now come back completely to the outside world.

---

**Reflection**

The learners' reflection can be stimulated by the following questions:

- Where did you feel your breath and how did it feel?
- What thoughts came up in you while you were focusing on your breath?
- Was it easy for you to return to the breath after a distraction?

---

### Planning for the Upcoming Practice Week

1. Perform one of the exercises learned so far (e.g., counting breaths, observing breath, or walking meditation) once a day.
2. Identify your stress situations. For this, observe your everyday life and whenever stress arises, take a step back and observe the situation from the outside. What was the trigger for the emerging stress? What did the stress trigger in you? And how do you notice that you are currently stressed? How does stress manifest itself on a physical, but also on a mental level? Note the stress situations as well as your perception of these on a physical and mental level.

## Minute of Silence

| | Stressful situations in everyday life | Meditation exercise |
|---|---|---|
| Monday | Trigger: | |
| | Physical experience | |
| | Mental experience | |
| Tuesday | Trigger: | |
| | Physical experience | |
| | Mental experience | |
| Wednesday | Trigger: | |
| | Physical experience | |
| | Mental experience | |
| Thursday | Trigger: | |
| | Physical experience | |
| | Mental experience | |
| Friday | Trigger: | |
| | Physical experience | |
| | Mental experience | |
| Saturday | Trigger:: | |
| | Physical experience | |
| | Mental experience | |
| Sunday | Trigger:: | |
| | Physical experience | |
| | Mental experience | |

# References

Killingsworth, M. A., & Gilbert, D. T. (2010). A wandering mind is an unhappy mind. *Science, 330*(6006), 932. https://doi.org/10.1126/science.1192439.

Späth, T., & Bao, S. Y. (2011). *Shaolin—Das Geheimnis der inneren Stärke*. Gräfe und Unzer.

# 7

# Course Unit 4: Body Perception—The Key to Emotions

**Goals**

- Improvement of body perception
- Improvement of concentration performance
- Improvement of emotion perception
- Relaxation

**Content: The importance of body perception**
Body perception is important to be aware of internal bodily processes. Knowledge of internal bodily processes enables the regulation of emotions. Body perception can be improved through psychoeducation and trained through simple exercises.

**Procedure:**

- Minute of silence
- Recapitulation of the last exercise week
- Psychoeducation
- Exercise 1: Observing the breath
- Reflection on Exercise 1
- Story "The Monk and the Samurai"
- Exercise 2: Body Scan
- Reflection on Exercise 2
- Planning of the upcoming exercise week
- Minute of silence

**Exercise 1: Observing the breath**

- Close eyes and feel into the body
- Focus on breath and use it to stay present with attention

© The Author(s), under exclusive license to Springer-Verlag GmbH, DE, part of Springer Nature 2024
D. Jekauc et al., *Mindfulness Training in Sport*,
https://doi.org/10.1007/978-3-662-68804-5_7

84 D. Jekauc et al.

- Observe breath without directly influencing it, and find own rhythm
- Accept mental drifting and return to breath

**Exercise 2: Body Scan**

- Sequentially direct attention to individual body parts (toes, feet, lower legs, thighs, stomach, back, shoulders, arms, hands, fingers, neck, and face)
- Perceive all physical sensations.
- Feel into the whole body once again

**Homework:**

1. Perform one of the two exercises once a day.
2. Ask yourself three times a day how you are physically feeling.

## Body perception—the key to emotions

### A Minute of Silence

Each course unit begins with a minute of silence to arrive in the here and now.

### Body Perception

Regarding what we perceive in and about ourselves, a distinction is made between the levels of perception of thoughts and body (Fig. 7.1). Body perception is an indicator of all mental processes and it helps to feel what is going on inside us. Training body perception develops an awareness of our own physical processes, because much of what happens in our body often goes unnoticed in our hectic everyday life. Body perception is a skill that we have lost in the course of our increasingly hectic and digitized life. However, the more subtle physical signals sometimes convey very important information about our physical and mental condition. The body also plays an important role in the perception of emotions, as all emotions manifest themselves in it. At the same time, however, the body is also capable of regulating mental processes, i.e., it is both an indicator and a regulator of all mental processes for us.

A well-developed body perception is therefore a prerequisite for being able to regulate oneself well. There is a "trick" where you force yourself to put on a friendly face and possibly smile for a few minutes when you're in a bad mood. Research over the past decades provides evidence that a physical reaction is not only an expression of an emotion, but that emotions can also be systematically influenced by deliberate physical expression. Physical

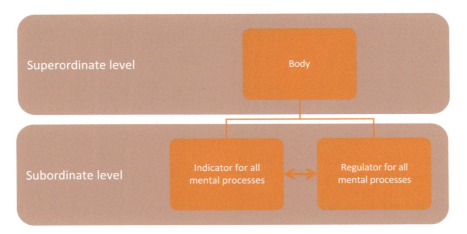

Fig. 7.1 Levels of Perception

expression and the subjective experience of an emotion influence each other. Conscious smiling can trigger positive emotions and thus regulate one's own emotions. The positive influence of body posture and facial expressions can also be used in sports. A dominant body posture, for example, can not only influence one's own perception, but also the perception of teammates and opponents. The emotions that become perceptible to others and opponents through mirroring can trigger cognitive and affective reactions in them. This applies to both team and individual sports. If a team celebrates a point win particularly, the entire team's self-confidence is positively influenced. Body postures and any other physical and externally perceptible manifestation of emotions can be part of the competition strategy. Just think of the Haka dance of the New Zealand rugby team, which wants to evoke fear in the opponent. Conscious perception of physical processes is the first step in building good body language.

**Report from Research**
- **Localization in the Brain:** The perception of emotions can be assigned to a specific area in the brain, the insular cortex. When emotions are actively perceived, an increased activity of the insula can be observed. This also makes it possible to train the abilities of body perception through repeated practice (Craig, 2002).
- **Relevance in Sports:** In sports, trained body perception can generate a positive influence on performance. Non-verbal behavior in sports, e.g. body posture, can act both as a result and as a predictor in relation to performance. This means that certain body postures or facial expressions can

influence both oneself and one's own team, as well as the opponents (Furley & Schweizer, 2020).

The ability of body perception can be trained with simple exercises and helps to regulate oneself. Because we can only do this if we know how we are doing. One of these helpful exercises is called "Observing Breath".

## Practical Exercises and Reflection
## Exercise 1: Observing Breath

### Background Information
Starting position: Upright, but comfortable sitting
Duration: 12–13 min
Benefit: Training of concentration, which is a necessary resource for meditation and subsequent mindfulness exercises, as well as the generation of a relaxation effect

### Instructions for Implementation
In this meditation, the focus should be on the breath. First, you should find a sitting position in which you can sit comfortably for a long time without having to move around. To calm the thoughts and feelings, it can be helpful to first bring the body to rest. So find a posture that is comfortable and stable and allows you to keep your back straight. Not rigid or tense, but in a way that you can breathe easily and naturally into your stomach and all parts of the body can be well supplied with blood. Now slowly close your eyes and bring your attention to the present, to the here and now. Find out what there is to discover here. Feel what your body feels like, are there certain sensations or pains? And where is the body relaxed and relaxed? Pay attention to the sounds around you. And what feelings are moving you inside? Fear or tension, hope, affection? And which thoughts are pushing themselves into the foreground? All of this belongs to you and your life: sensations, feelings, thoughts. And now, in the midst of all this, become aware of the fact that you are breathing. Or in other words: that breathing is happening. We want to use the movement of the breath to practice staying present with our attention. How do you perceive the breath? A coolness at the back of the throat when inhaling? The warmth of the exhaled air, a tingling? The movement of your chest, the stomach, which rises and falls?

Feel your breath, but try not to change or control it. Just become aware of it, and let it find its own rhythm. Your body breathes by itself. For the next ten minutes, just feel each breath as it flows in and out. No matter where it makes itself noticeable, in the nose, in the throat, in the stomach.

## 7 Course Unit 4: Body Perception—The Key to Emotions 87

Feel each breath completely. You will notice that your thoughts wander. Plans or memories distract you. Don't get upset about it! Each time you become aware of it, look at these thoughts from the outside. Let them go again. Return to your breath. Imagine how the breath brings oxygen into your body, which is absorbed into the blood in the lungs, and is distributed throughout your body with each beat of your heart.

And now slowly turn your attention back to your surroundings, pay attention to the sounds in the room that surrounds you. Feel the air on your skin and the light that shimmers through your eyelids. And when you are ready, gently open your eyes again, now fully return to the outside world.

---

**Reflection**

The learners' reflection can be stimulated by the following questions:

- How did you perceive your breath? Where did you feel it?
- How well were you able to stay focused on your breath?
- Did many thoughts go through your head? Or have the thoughts perhaps wandered less often?
- When you drifted away from your breath, what kind of thoughts came up in you?
- Were you able to return to your breath after you had drifted away?
- How did the exercise feel compared to the previous week?

---

### Story for Reflection: The Monk and the Samurai

"A young Zen monk, as the story goes in Shaolin, was tasked with delivering an important letter. On his way, he had to cross a bridge, but when he reached it, an experienced samurai was standing there. This samurai had sworn to challenge the first hundred men who wanted to cross the bridge to a duel. He had already killed ninety-nine. The monk asked the samurai to let him pass because he had a very important letter to deliver. At the same time, he promised to come back and fight the samurai as soon as he had delivered the letter. The samurai hesitated at first, but then agreed, and the monk was able to continue his journey. After he had delivered the letter, the monk, certain that he would soon have to die, sought out his master to say goodbye. "I have to fight a great samurai, and I have never held a sword in my hands. He will surely kill me." "Indeed," replied the master, "you will die, for you have no chance of winning. So I will teach you the best way to die: You raise your sword above your head, keep your eyes closed and wait. If you feel something cold on your crown, that is death. At that moment, you let your arms and everything you believe you possess fall. That's all."

## 88    D. Jekauc et al.

The monk bowed to his master and returned to the bridge where the samurai was already waiting for him. The two prepared for battle. The monk did exactly as his master had advised him. He took his sword in both hands, raised it above his head, closed his eyes, and waited completely motionless. This surprised and deeply confused the samurai, as his opponent's posture did not reflect any fear. Becoming suspicious, he cautiously approached the monk, who stood completely calm, focused solely on his crown. The samurai thought: This man is obviously extraordinarily strong. He had the courage to return and fight me. The monk still stood motionless. The samurai became increasingly puzzled, and suddenly he was sure: This man is undoubtedly an excellent warrior. He adopts an attacking position from the start and then even closes his eyes!

The monk had by now completely forgotten the samurai. Completely focused on following his master's advice and dying with dignity, he stood there, detached and freed from all worldly things. The samurai had meanwhile come to the certainty that he would be cut in two at the slightest movement on his part, and finally began to speak in a whimpering voice: "Please have mercy on me, and do not kill me. I thought I was a master of swordsmanship, but now I know that I have met a true master today. Please accept me as your student, and teach me the way of the sword." (quoted from Moestl, 2008, p. 89ff.). *quote translated from German*

### Discussion
In addition to the learners' interpretations, the following approaches can also be discussed (in the group):

- The monk radiated calmness during the confrontation with the experienced samurai. The story illustrates that through calmness—even in the face of serious things like death—emotions like fear recede into the background.
- Calmness not only affects one's own emotions, but also the opponent or the confronting situation: The samurai felt suddenly inferior in the face of the monk's calmness and considered the monk a strong master. In the context of sports, this can mean that by radiating calmness, one demonstrates superiority.
- While he initially had been afraid of the samurai, the monk ultimately completely forgets him, as he is so focused on himself. A third possible transfer to the sports context lies in this very concentration on oneself. If one is too preoccupied with the opponent, one is distracted from

## 7 Course Unit 4: Body Perception—The Key to Emotions 89

one's own needs and may be inadvertently plunged into a state of fear. Therefore, it is more sensible to stay with oneself.

### Exercise 2: Body Scan

**Background Information**
Starting position: Lying position (optional: comfortable seat)
Duration: 12–13 min
Benefits: Conscious perception of physical processes; Side effect: Increase in relaxation and practising concentration

Another exercise for training body perception is the body scan, in which all body parts are perceived intensively one after the other. The following text can either be read aloud by the course leader or read silently by oneself.

**Instructions for Execution**
Lie down on a mat or a soft, comfortable surface and find a cozy position. Just make sure that your body parts, such as your legs, do not touch each other. If you prefer, sit upright but still comfortably on a chair. In case you want to perform the exercise while sitting, place your feet loosely on the floor and put your hands in your lap or let them hang loosely beside your body. Close your eyes and take several deep breaths to calm down.

Now direct your attention to your body. What do you perceive? Is your body evenly on the pad? Do you feel pressure at some points or the clothing on your skin? Try to perceive every facet of your body, both the skin surface and the sensations inside. Start with your feet. Feel how your feet touch the ground. Be fully aware of every part of your feet, your heels, your soles, your toes, and your instep. If you feel tension or another feeling, engage with this sensation. Can you dedicate yourself to this sensation without judging it, just accepting it as it is? Then move your attention to your lower legs, feel into them, feel the calves and the shins. Engage with each sensation as long as you want and if your attention turns to another part of your body, allow this. If your thoughts distract you, be aware that this is okay. Just try to bring your attention back to your body. Next, feel into your knees, then into your thighs. Can you feel how they touch the ground on which you are sitting or lying? Then feel into your stomach. Breathe deeply into your stomach. The abdominal wall rises and falls with each breath, try to feel this exactly. Next, your attention moves to your back. Can you feel where your back touches the pad? Is your back relaxed, are your shoulders hanging loosely down? Try not to judge the sensations you perceive. Next, turn to your facial muscles. Are they relaxed? How do you perceive your lower jaw, rather loose or tense? Let the muscles relax. You can also lay your eyelids very loosely on top of each other. Finally, feel into your arms. Feel where your arms touch the pad, feel every part of your arms, the upper arms, the elbows, the forearms, and finally your fingers.

When you have scanned all parts of your body with your attention, get ready to come back to the here and now. Take a few deep breaths, gently move your fingers and toes, move your arms and legs, stretch and open your eyes again.

---

**Reflection**

The learners' reflection can be stimulated by the following questions:

- How well were you able to focus on your body and the individual body parts?
- Which body part were you able to perceive particularly well?
- Did your body feel warm/cold?
- Could you feel a tingling or other sensations?
- Do you feel different than before the exercise?

---

**Planning for the Upcoming Exercise Week**

1. Perform a daily body scan or a breathing meditation in a quiet environment for about 10–15 min. Try to practice the exercises at the same time of day if possible.
2. Ask yourself three times a day, e.g., after getting up, at work during the break, or in the evening before going to sleep, how you are physically. Try to perceive all physical sensations as exactly as possible. Record the physical perceptions in your notebook.

## Minute of Silence

| | Physical sensations | Meditation exercise |
|---|---|---|
| **Monday** | | |
| Morning | | |
| Lunch | | |
| Evening | | |
| **Tuesday** | | |
| Morning | | |
| Lunch | | |
| Evening | | |
| **Wednesday** | | |
| Morning | | |
| Lunch | | |
| Evening | | |
| **Thursday** | | |
| Morning | | |
| Lunch | | |
| Evening | | |
| **Friday** | | |
| Morning | | |
| Lunch | | |
| Evening | | |
| **Saturday** | | |
| Morning | | |
| Lunch | | |
| Evening | | |
| **Sunday** | | |
| Morning | | |
| Lunch | | |
| Evening | | |

# References

Craig, A. D. (2002). How do you feel? Interoception: The sense of the physiological condition of the body. *Nature Reviews Neuroscience, 3,* 655–666. https://doi.org/10.1038/nrn894.

Furley, P. & Schweizer, G. (2020). Body language in sport. In G. Tenenbaum, & R. C. Eklund (eds.), *Handbook of Sport Psychology* (4th ed., S. 1201–1219). Wiley. https://doi.org/10.1002/9781119568124.ch59.

Moestl, B. (2008). *Shaolin. Du musst nicht kämpfen, um zu siegen.* Knaur.

# 8

# Course Unit 5: Perception of Thoughts

**Goals**

- Observation of one's own thoughts
- Deepening of concentration skills

**Content: The Power of Thoughts**
Our thoughts influence how we feel. Especially when these thoughts have negative effects on our mood, it is important to break them. To do this, one can perceive and select one's thoughts from the position of an external observer, determining which of these thoughts are helpful and justified.

**Procedure:**

- Minute of silence
- Recapitulation of the last practice week
- Psychoeducation
- Exercise 1: Observing breath with labeling
- Reflection of the 1st exercise
- Story "The Story with the Hammer"
- Exercise 2: Observing thoughts
- Reflection of the 2nd exercise
- Planning of the upcoming practice week

**Exercise 1: Observing breath with labeling**

- Close eyes
- Participants focus on their breathing
- Emerging thoughts are named (labeled)

© The Author(s), under exclusive license to Springer-Verlag GmbH, DE, part of Springer Nature 2024
D. Jekauc et al., *Mindfulness Training in Sport*,
https://doi.org/10.1007/978-3-662-68804-5_8

## Exercise 2: Observing thoughts

- Focus on thoughts
- Name emerging moods and bodily sensations and direct attention to them
- Give a name to emerging thoughts
- Do not actively manipulate thoughts, just observe them

**Homework:**

1. Perform one of the two exercises once a day.
2. Ask yourself three times a day: What's going through my mind? Note down your thoughts and their origin.

## Perception of Thoughts

### A Minute of Silence

Each course unit begins with a minute of silence to arrive in the here and now.

### The Power of Thoughts

Every day, an estimated 80,000 thoughts go through each of our heads. Many thoughts repeat themselves, some make sense and others are irrelevant or inappropriate. However, they all have in common that they influence how we feel. Thoughts follow the principle of association. One jumps from one wave of thought to the next, creating entire chains of thought. When thoughts become automatic and occur more often in our heads, these chains become increasingly difficult to break. Additionally, the more emotional a thought is, the harder it becomes to interrupt this flow of thoughts. You can imagine it like standing at a stream where not too much water flows through the stream bed, so you can cross it without difficulty. However, the wider the water becomes, the more likely you are to wobble when crossing—until eventually you have no chance of crossing the river. Sometimes, however, with thoughts and emotions, it is exactly this "crossing" or interruption that is important and necessary, especially when our thoughts influence negatively our mood. To free oneself from the negative mood, it is then important to stop the carousel of thoughts and to be in the here and now.

In addition, one tends to see our thoughts as truth. What is often forgotten, however, is that perception, which is a basis of thought, is constantly deceived. Therefore, one constructs a mental reality through an interpretation of what one perceives. In addition, we supplement our perception with expectations based on our knowledge and experiences. This is also the case with athletes. Each competition is associated with a certain expectation. Do I estimate my chances of winning as high or rather low? This expectation of winning then influences the emotional state during the competition, which does not always allow for peak performance.

Interrupting the flow of thoughts and not taking one's thoughts too seriously, however, does not mean pushing away or ignoring thoughts. Instead, one should become aware of what is going on in one's own head and make a decision about which thoughts have a right to exist. So one perceives one's thoughts very precisely and selects. Sometimes it can also help to observe one's thoughts from a certain distance, perhaps even to give the thought a name in order to be able to classify it better. When observing thoughts closely, it is always important to keep in mind: Just because a thought is there, it does not have to correspond to the truth. You are not what you think! With this knowledge and a selection of thoughts, one can take away their power. The flow of thoughts can thus become a stream of thoughts again, which one can cross without effort.

Exactly this ability to conquer the flow of thoughts is a basis for emotional strength. This applies equally to sports and everyday life. Nobody enjoys being in a bad mood all day long. Often enough, thoughts about negative mood pull us into a downward spiral of brooding. This can not only end negatively for our daily actions, but also for performance in sports. A common phrase in coach interviews after the game is: "The team played with their heads". This means that the players brooded over something, could not cross the flow of thoughts, which resulted in them not being able to perform their actual performance.

To prevent this from happening in sports or everyday life, it is so important to listen to oneself, collect one's thoughts, understand them and consider which of them one really wants to give the power to be influenced by.

## Practical Exercises and Reflection
## Exercise 1: Observing Breath with Labeling

### Background Information
Starting position: Upright, but comfortable sitting
Duration: 15 min
Benefits: Training of concentration, which is a necessary resource for meditating and for subsequent mindfulness exercises, as well as the generation of a relaxation effect, training of conscious perception of thoughts

## Instructions for Execution

To focus on your breath, find a sitting position where you can sit comfortably for an extended period. Calm your body by finding a comfortable and stable posture where you can breathe easily and naturally into your belly. If you like, close your eyes and focus your attention on the here and now. Feel what your body feels like. Are there specific sensations, tensions, or pains, and where is the body relaxed and at ease? Pay attention to the sounds around you and the feelings that move you internally. Fear or tension? Hope, affection? And which thoughts and expectations push themselves to the forefront? All of this belongs to you and your life: sensations, feelings, and thoughts. Now consciously realize that you are breathing alongside all these sensations. Use the movement of the breath to practice staying present with your attention. Observe your breath very closely, how do you perceive it? A coolness at the back of your throat when inhaling? The warmth of the exhaled air? A tingling? The movement of your chest? The belly rising and falling? Feel your breath, but try not to change or control it. Just be aware of it and let it find its own rhythm. For the next ten minutes, simply feel your breath as it flows in and out. No matter where it makes itself noticeable: in the nose, throat, belly. You will notice that your thoughts wander. Plans or memories distract you. If, while following your breath, thoughts arise that capture you and you lose yourself in them—these can be images or words, memories or plans—then give these thoughts a name. Call them, for example, simply "planning" or "remembering". Usually, these thoughts dissolve when you become aware of them. Your attention works similarly to sunlight on fog. The thoughts disappear and you can return to your breath. Sometimes, if it is a very intense, strong thought, it will not disappear immediately. Then simply continue to name it "remembering", "planning", or "thinking" until it disappears. And then return to your breath. Imagine how the breath brings oxygen into your body, which is absorbed into the blood in the lungs and distributed throughout your body with every beat of your heart.

When you are ready, slowly direct your attention back to your surroundings and prepare to open your eyes again.

---

### Reflection

The learners' reflection can be stimulated by the following questions.

- How did you perceive your breath? Where did you feel it?
- How well were you able to stay focused on your breathing?

## 8  Course Unit 5: Perception of Thoughts

- Did you have many thoughts going through your head? Or did your thoughts perhaps wander less often?
- If you drifted away from your breath, were you able to find a name for your thoughts and was one category particularly frequent?
- Were you able to return to your breath after you had drifted away?
- How did the exercise feel compared to the previous week?

### Story for Reflection: "The Story with the Hammer"

"A man wants to hang up a picture. He has the nail, but not the hammer. The neighbor has one. So our man decides to go over and borrow it. But then he has a doubt: What if the neighbor doesn't want to lend me the hammer? Yesterday he only greeted me so briefly. Maybe he was in a hurry. But maybe the hurry was just a pretense, and he has something against me. And what? I haven't done anything to him; he's imagining something. If someone wanted to borrow a tool from me, I would give it to him immediately. And why not him? How can one deny a fellow human being such a simple favor? People like this guy poison one's life. And then he even imagines that I am dependent on him. Just because he has a hammer. Now I've really had enough.—And so he storms over, rings the bell, the neighbor opens, but before he can say "Good day", our man yells at him: "Keep your hammer, you brute!" (Watzlawick, 2021, p. 37 f.). *quote translated from German*

### Discussion

In addition to the learners' interpretations, the following approaches can also be discussed (in the group):

- The man in the story already starts thinking about the outcome of the upcoming situation and begins to doubt. His ideas about the course of the situation move further and further away from a realistically expected scenario. Even before anything negative has happened, he assumes the worst and ultimately denies himself the chance of help in the form of the hammer. It is not sensible to worry too much about the course of an event, e.g., a competition, because one cannot know what will actually happen.
- The man gets tangled up in a chain of thoughts, where he moves from one negative idea to the next. One can also get into a downward spiral of negative thoughts in a competition, where one negative thought directly

triggers the next. These chains of thoughts should not have too much power over us, i.e., they should not become reality.

- Finally, the man addresses the neighbor as if the thoughts on the way to him were actually facts that had occurred. We create our own reality, which may not correspond to the reality of others.

## Exercise 2: Observing Thoughts

Starting position: Comfortable and stable sitting position
Duration: 15 min
Benefit: Conscious perception of one's own thoughts

### Instructions for execution

In this meditation, the flow of our thoughts should be observed. Find a comfortable sitting position again that allows you to breathe freely. Now first focus on your breath. Observe your breath closely, try to feel its beginning, its middle, and its end. Also pay attention to how you perceive it. Is it short or long, soft or hard, strong or weak. If, while you are observing your breath, certain body sensations or noises or moods become noticeable, then let go of the breath for a moment and name them. Give them a name and devote the same mindful attention to them as you did to your breath before. We now also want to include our thoughts. If, while you are following your breath, thoughts arise, capture you and you lose yourself in them, these can be images or words, memories or plans, then give these thoughts a name. Call them, for example, simply "Planning" or "Remembering". Normally these thoughts dissolve when you become aware of them. Therefore, allow your thoughts and try to notice which thoughts are going through your head without actively influencing them. Your attention works similarly to sunlight on fog. The thoughts disappear, but sometimes, if it is a very intense, strong thought, it will not disappear immediately. Then simply continue to name it. Kindly and gently, as "Remembering", "Planning" or "Thinking". Think the thought to the end, trace your thoughts back: Where did this thought just come from? Follow it as long as it dissolves. You take on the role of someone who observes thoughts like clouds in the sky.

And now you can slowly direct your attention back to your surroundings. Pay attention to the noises and the space that surrounds you. Feel the air on your skin and the light that shimmers through your eyelids. And when you are ready, gently open your eyes and now fully return to the outside world.

## Reflection

The learners' reflection can be stimulated by the following questions:

- Did many thoughts go through your head? Or have the thoughts perhaps drifted off less often?
- If you drifted away from your breath, were you able to find a name for your thoughts and was one category particularly common?
- Were you able to trace your thoughts back and observe them without judgment, without actively steering them?
- How did the exercise feel compared to the previous exercise?

## Planning the upcoming practice week

1. Perform one of the two exercises (observing breath with labeling/observing thoughts) daily. Record your meditation experiences.
2. Ask yourself the question three times a day: What's going through my head? Record your thoughts and their origin.

## Minute of Silence

| | Thoughts and their origin | Meditation exercise |
|---|---|---|
| **Monday** | | |
| Morning | | |
| Lunch | | |
| Evening | | |
| **Tuesday** | | |
| Morning | | |
| Lunch | | |
| Evening | | |
| **Wednesday** | | |
| Morning | | |
| Lunch | | |
| Evening | | |
| **Thursday** | | |
| Morning | | |
| Lunch | | |
| Evening | | |
| **Friday** | | |
| Morning | | |
| Lunch | | |
| Evening | | |
| **Saturday** | | |
| Morning | | |
| Lunch | | |
| Evening | | |
| **Sunday** | | |
| Morning | | |
| Lunch | | |
| Evening | | |

## References

Watzlawick, P. (2021). *Anleitung zum Unglücklichsein.* Piper.

# 9

# Course Unit 6: Perception of Feelings

**Goals**

- Training of conscious perception of thoughts and feelings
- Reflection of one's own mental model

**Content: Mental models and the inner observer**
Each of us thinks, feels, and acts based on a structure that is built up through experiences and values, and that makes it easier in everyday life to perceive and classify information. This structure is called a mental model. A value-free observer attitude can be adopted for the reflection of the mental model. This allows the patterns behind thoughts and feelings to be understood, they can be broken through, and one gets to know oneself better.

**Procedure**

- Minute of silence
- Recapitulation of the last practice week
- Psychoeducation
- Exercise 1: Observing breath with labeling
- Reflection of Exercise 1
- Story "Two monks on the shore"
- Exercise 2: Observing feelings
- Reflection of Exercise 2
- Planning of the upcoming practice week
- Minute of silence

© The Author(s), under exclusive license to Springer-Verlag GmbH, DE, part of Springer Nature 2024
D. Jekauc et al., *Mindfulness Training in Sport*,
https://doi.org/10.1007/978-3-662-68804-5_9

> **Exercise 1: Observing breath with labeling**
>
> - Close eyes
> - Participants focus on their breathing
> - Emerging thoughts are named (labeled)
>
> **Exercise 2: Observing feelings**
>
> - Perception of tensions in the body
> - Observation of one's own mood
> - Focus on the breath
> - Emerging thoughts and sensations are observed, their origin traced back and named
> - Return to the breath as thoughts and sensations subside
>
> **Homework**
>
> 1. Perform one of the two exercises daily.
> 2. Become aware of what is currently going well in your life. Often the beautiful moments in everyday life are overlooked, so be particularly aware of them this week.

## Perceiving Feelings

### A Minute of Silence

Each program unit begins with a minute of silence to arrive in the here and now.

### Getting to Know the Mental Model Thanks to the Inner Observer

We are all limited in our perception and it is not possible for us to perceive every detail of reality. Instead, everyone has an individual filter that determines what we see. This filter can be described as a mental model: a structure on the basis of which relationships are recognized and decisions are made, and which can even influence our behavior. This filter is constructed through life experiences, perceptions, and the understanding of the world, which is significantly influenced by values and goals. The mental model is an automatic mechanism that cannot be turned on or off and through which new information is filtered and classified. As already known from the autopilot, automations make our everyday life easier, but there is always the danger that the emergence and perceptions of thoughts, feelings, values, and patterns of action are no longer reflected.

# 9 Course Unit 6: Perception of Feelings 103

In order to understand and reflect on one's own mental model, one can take a look behind the scenes with the help of mindfulness. What triggers certain thoughts and feelings or patterns of action? If one considers this aspect under the analogy of streams of thought, this reflection means not to be carried away by thoughts and to evaluate them, but to stand on the bank of the river and thus adopt a value-free observer attitude. So you perceive thoughts and feelings with distance to yourself and do not identify with your own sensations.

This value-free observer attitude is often described by the inner observer, a system that precisely registers what is happening inside us. Slipping into the role of the inner observer can help not to let thoughts become habits and to detach the thought patterns that already exist from their habits. Especially at the beginning, it can be difficult to take on the role of the inner observer. But as with other mindfulness practices, with repeated practice day by day, it becomes easier to face your thoughts and feelings without judgment. And the practice will pay off. You get to know your thought patterns and can understand what triggers negative thoughts, for example. With this knowledge, you can turn a raging river of thoughts into a calm stream and break the cycle of negative emotions. Through this process of distancing, you get to know and understand yourself better and thus find your way back to yourself.

## Practical Exercises and Reflection

### Exercise 1: Observing Breath with Labeling

**Background Information**
Starting position: Upright, but comfortable seat
Duration: 17 min
Benefits: Training of concentration, which is a necessary resource for meditating and for subsequent mindfulness exercises, as well as the generation of a relaxation effect, training of conscious perception of thoughts

### Instructions for Implementation
In order for you to focus on your breath, find a sitting position in which you can sit comfortably for a long time. Bring your body to rest by finding a comfortable and stable posture in which you can breathe easily and naturally into your stomach. If you like, close your eyes and direct your attention to the here and now. Feel what your body feels like. Are there certain sensations, tensions or pains and where is the body relaxed and relaxed? Pay attention to

the sounds around you and to the feelings that move you inside. Fear or tension? Hope, affection? And what thoughts and expectations come to the fore? All this belongs to you and your life: sensations, feelings, and thoughts. Now consciously realize that you are breathing in addition to all these sensations. Use the movement of the breath to practice staying in the present with your attention. Observe your breath very closely, how do you perceive it? A coolness at the back of your throat when inhaling? The warmth of the exhaled air? A tingling sensation? The movement of your chest? The belly rising and falling? Feel your breath, but try not to change or control it. Just become aware of it and let it find its own rhythm. For the next ten minutes, just feel your breath as it flows in and out. No matter where it makes itself noticeable: in the nose, in the throat, in the stomach. You will notice that your thoughts wander. Plans or memories distract you. If, while following your breath, thoughts arise that capture you and you lose yourself in them - these can be images or words, memories or plans - then give these thoughts a name. Call them, for example, simply "planning" or "remembering". Usually, these thoughts dissolve when you become aware of them. Your attention works similarly to sunlight on fog. The thoughts disappear and you can return to your breath. Sometimes, if it is a very intense, strong thought, it will not disappear immediately. Then just continue to name it "remember", "plan" or "think" until it disappears. And then return to your breath. Imagine how the breath brings oxygen into your body, which is absorbed into the blood in the lungs and distributed throughout your body with every beat of your heart.

When you are ready, slowly direct your attention back to your surroundings and prepare to open your eyes again.

---

### Reflection

The learners' reflection can be stimulated by the following questions:

- How did you perceive your breath? Where did you feel it?
- How well were you able to keep your concentration on your breathing?
- Did many thoughts go through your head? Or have the thoughts perhaps wandered less often?
- If you drifted away from your breath, were you able to find a name for your thoughts and was there a category that occurred particularly often?
- Were you able to return to your breath after you had drifted away?
- How did the exercise feel compared to the previous week?

## 9 Course Unit 6: Perception of Feelings 105

### Story for Reflection: Two Monks at the Shore

"A young and an old monk are walking along a path. They come to a river with a strong current. As they prepare to cross it, they see a pretty young woman who can't reach the other shore. She notices the monks and asks them for help. The old monk carries her across the river on his shoulder. She thanks him and goes her way. The young monk is angry. Really angry.

Hours later, he is still angry. The old monk asks him what's wrong. "As monks, we are not allowed to touch young women! How could you carry her across the river?" The old monk replies: "I left the woman on the shore hours ago, but it seems you are still carrying her around with you." (quoted from Alizadeh, 2019, p. 175f.). *quote translated from German*

### Discussion

In addition to the learners' interpretations, the following approaches can also be discussed (in the group):

- The young monk cannot let go of thoughts that collide with expectations, values, and ideas of his mental model and broods over them. The thoughts develop into negative emotions. He is no longer in the here and now.
- The older monk reflects on his values and adapts them to the situation. It is important to reflect on and re-evaluate fixed thought patterns.
- In sports too, it is important not to carry mistakes made through the competition (like the young monk carries the woman in his thoughts), but to put them aside. Mistakes are always relative.

### Exercise 2: Observing the Feelings

#### Background Information

Starting position: Comfortable and stable posture
Duration: 17 minutes
Benefit: Conscious perception of one's own feelings

#### Instructions for Execution

In this meditation, we want to observe not only our physical sensations but also our feelings. First, find a posture that is comfortable and stable, allowing you to keep your body still for about 20 minutes, with a straight back and so that you can breathe freely. And then, let your eyes slowly close. Now first of all, become aware of your body. How does it feel? Let the day pass by you once again. If you feel any tension in your body, try to let it become soft and relaxed. Now let the muscles around your eyes soften and relax your jaw muscles. Also relax your shoulders, your arms, and your hands. Relax your chest and your abdominal muscles, let your stomach be completely relaxed and soft. Consider what mood you are in right now. Are you, for example, excited, sleepy, or calm? Simply acknowledge your mood without judging it. And now focus your attention again on your inhaling and exhaling. Feel your breath without influencing it. Let it find its own rhythm.

As you focus on your breath, certain sensations may arise in your body, such as itching or tingling, palpitations, or pain. And then you might also discover certain feelings within you. Perhaps you are happy or sad, worried or amused. Name these physical sensations and these feelings. And see what happens to your feelings as you observe them. Do they stay the same? Do they get stronger? Or do they disappear? Stay with your physical sensations and your feelings as long as they are strong. And when they weaken, return to your breath and be aware of how it flows in and out.

If you notice that your thoughts are wandering, that they are getting lost in fantasies or memories, then simply let them go and return to your breath or to the sensations that are present right now. Be aware of the feelings and sensations you have right now. Observe them with a friendly, mindful attention and when they weaken, return to your breath. And again and again, when your thoughts wander, simply let them go and gently and kindly bring your attention back to your breath or your sensations. And now slowly bring your attention back to your surroundings. Pay attention to the sounds and the space around you, feel the air on your skin and the light shimmering through your eyelids. And when you are ready, gently open your eyes and fully return to the outside world.

---

### Reflection

The learners' reflection can be stimulated by the following questions:

- Were you able to perceive and name physical sensations and feelings?
- What happened to these while and after you named them?
- Was it easy for you to let go of emerging thoughts and return to your breath?
- Were some thoughts and sensations stronger than others, so that you had to stay with them longer?

---

## Planning for the Upcoming Practice Week

1. Perform one of the two exercises daily.
2. Be aware of what is going well in your life right now. Often we overlook the beautiful moments in everyday life, so be particularly aware of them this week.

## Minute of Silence

| | Beautiful moments in everyday life | Meditation exercise |
|---|---|---|
| Monday | | |
| Tuesday | | |
| Wednesday | | |
| Thursday | | |
| Friday | | |
| Saturday | | |
| Sunday | | |

# Reference

Alizadeh, M. (2019). *Starkes weiches Herz. Wie Mut und Liebe unsere Welt verändern können.* Ullstein.

# 10

# Course Unit 7: Promoting Positive Feelings

**Goals**
- Deepening concentration ability by observing the breath
- Perception of emotions
- Activation of positive emotions

**Content: Emotions**
Emotions have a strong influence on decisions and motivation. Therefore, it is important to master the regulation of emotions. Mindfulness helps by teaching to accept perceived feelings without judgment and thus being able to let go of them more quickly.

**Procedure**

- Minute of silence
- Recapitulation of the last practice week
- Psychoeducation
- Exercise 1: Observing breath with labeling
- Reflection of Exercise 1
- Story "Two Wolves"
- Exercise 2: Activating positive emotions
- Reflection of Exercise 2
- Planning of the upcoming practice week
- Minute of silence

**Exercise 1: Observing breath with labeling**

- Close eyes
- Participants focus on their breathing
- Emerging thoughts are named (labeled)

© The Author(s), under exclusive license to Springer-Verlag GmbH, DE, part of Springer Nature 2024
D. Jekauc et al., *Mindfulness Training in Sport*,
https://doi.org/10.1007/978-3-662-68804-5_10

> **Exercise 2: Activating positive emotions**
>
> - Perceive and relax the body
> - Imagination of a positive event
> - Conscious perception of emotions
> - Accept and name emerging body sensations and thoughts
> - Return to the breath when feelings fade
>
> **Homework:**
>
> 1. Perform one of the two exercises once a day.
> 2. Note down three things you are grateful for every day.

## Promoting Positive Feelings

### A Minute of Silence

Each course unit begins with a minute of silence to arrive in the here and now.

### Emotions

As humans, we are equipped with many abilities, e.g., intelligence, the purpose of which is immediately clear to us. The purpose of emotions in our lives is not immediately apparent. However, emotions mark significant experiences in our lives. Only those matters that are important to us can become emotional for us. In this respect, emotions give our lives meaning. But emotions can also stand in our way and rob us of all our strength when they become too intense. Therefore, it is important to deal productively with emotions and use their power to master life's challenges.

Emotions have a number of functions in our lives. An important function is to assist in decision-making. Many of our decisions are influenced by emotions. Emotions provide a basis for evaluating whether something is good or bad for us, whether it is fun or unpleasant. Essentially, emotional processes provide a basis for decision-making, allowing us to compare things that are rationally difficult to compare. For example, we can decide whether we want to eat with a good friend or rather go rowing with other sports friends—simply because we have a feeling for what we would rather do, while it would be time-consuming to make a decision rationally.

The second function of emotions is social communication. Emotional expression is often a signal to other people. In general, emotions can also be understood as a non-verbal language that is very universal and plays an important role in the animal kingdom. The way we express our emotions influences other people in our environment, our teammates, our partners, and opponents.

The third function is to influence our thinking. When we are in a bad mood, we are more likely to have negative thoughts and see the world more negatively than when we are in a good mood. Our memory is also influenced by emotional factors. When we are in a bad mood, we are more likely to remember bad and negative events than when we are in a good mood. Thus, emotions also have a tendency to reinforce themselves or to maintain themselves at a high level.

Finally, it should be mentioned that emotions have a motivational function. We are naturally designed to seek out positive situations and avoid negative ones. Accordingly, our behavior is influenced by these emotional factors.

Due to the great influence of emotions on our everyday life, it is all the more important to know and be able to regulate our own emotions. This begins with consciously and differentiatedly perceiving one's emotions and accepting the experience of emotions. To be able to recognize the situational trigger of an emotion, it can help to give one's emotions a name. Through these methods, one can learn to escape the downward spiral of negative emotions. But with well-trained emotion regulation, one can also act in the other direction. Not only can negative emotions be mitigated, but positive emotions can also be intensified. We can also enhance positive emotions through our thoughts.

For competitive sports, emotions are of crucial importance because they have a great influence on performance. Competitive sports in itself is very emotional because a lot is at stake that is important to us. In decisive situations of a competition, emotions can spoil our plans and lead to an unwanted turn of the match. Therefore, emotional stability is considered a crucial prerequisite for performance.

## Practical exercises and reflection

### Exercise 1: Observing breath with labeling

#### Background information
Starting position: Upright, but comfortable sitting
Duration: 20 min
Benefits: Training of concentration, which is a necessary resource for meditating and for subsequent mindfulness exercises, as well as the generation of a relaxation effect, training of conscious perception of thoughts

## Instructions for Implementation

To focus on your breath, find a sitting position where you can sit comfortably for an extended period. Calm your body by finding a comfortable and stable posture where you can breathe easily and naturally into your stomach. If you like, close your eyes and focus your attention on the here and now. Feel what your body feels like. Are there specific sensations, tensions, or pains? Where is the body relaxed and at ease? Pay attention to the sounds around you and the feelings that move you internally. Fear or tension? Hope, affection? And what thoughts and expectations come to the fore? All of this belongs to you and your life: sensations, feelings, and thoughts. Now consciously realize that you are breathing alongside all these sensations. Use the movement of the breath to practice staying present with your attention. Observe your breath very closely, how do you perceive it? A coolness at the back of your throat when inhaling? The warmth of the exhaled air? A tingling? The movement of your chest? The stomach rising and falling? Feel your breath, but try not to change or control it. Just be aware of it and let it find its own rhythm. For the next ten minutes, simply feel your breath as it flows in and out. No matter where it makes itself noticeable: in the nose, in the throat, in the stomach. You will notice that your thoughts wander. Plans or memories distract you. If, while following your breath, thoughts arise that capture you and you lose yourself in them—these can be images or words, memories or plans—then give these thoughts a name. Call them, for example, simply "planning" or "remembering". Usually, these thoughts dissolve when you become aware of them. Your attention works similarly to sunlight on fog. The thoughts disappear and you can return to your breath. Sometimes, if it is a very intense, strong thought, it will not disappear immediately. Then simply continue to name it "remembering", "planning" or "thinking" until it disappears. And then return to your breath. Imagine how the breath brings oxygen into your body, which is absorbed into the blood in the lungs and distributed throughout your body with every beat of your heart.

When you are ready, slowly redirect your attention to your surroundings and prepare to open your eyes again.

### Reflection

The learners' reflection can be stimulated by the following questions:

- How did you perceive your breath? Where did you feel it?
- How well were you able to stay focused on your breathing?
- Did you have many thoughts going through your head? Or did your thoughts perhaps wander less often?

> - If you drifted away from your breath, were you able to find a name for your thoughts and was one category particularly frequent?
> - Were you able to return to your breath after you had drifted away?
> - How did the exercise feel compared to the previous week?

## Story for Reflection: The Two Wolves

"One evening, an old Cherokee Indian told his grandson about a battle that rages inside every human being. He said: 'My son, the battle is fought by two wolves that live inside each of us. One is evil. He is anger, envy, jealousy, worry, pain, greed, arrogance, self-pity, guilt, prejudice, feelings of inferiority, lies, false pride, and ego. The other is good. He is joy, peace, love, hope, serenity, humility, kindness, benevolence, affection, generosity, truth, compassion, and faith.' The grandson thought about his grandfather's words for a while and then asked: 'Which of the two wolves wins?' The old Cherokee replied: 'The one you feed.'" (quoted from Merkl 2022, p. 40). *quote translated from German*

## Discussion

In addition to the learners' interpretations, the following approaches can also be discussed (in the group):

- The battle between the two wolves represents the battle one fights with oneself. There are always positive as well as negative thoughts and characteristics within one. However, we actively decide which of the two opposites prevails, which wolf we feed.
- The prerequisite for co-deciding is the awareness of what is inside us and what is going on, which symbolic battles the wolves are fighting.
- One way to move on the continuum between good and evil towards the good is to cultivate positive emotions—to feed the good wolf. This means that one consciously generates positive emotions, for example, by remembering a sporting success. The side you focus on becomes stronger and influences your own thinking and actions. If you actively integrate positive thoughts into your everyday life and feed them, this side builds up in you.

## Exercise 2: Activating Positive Emotions

### Background Information

Starting position: Comfortable and stable sitting posture
Duration: 20 min
   Benefits: Imagining pleasant experiences and conscious perception of one's own feelings

## Instructions for Execution

In this meditation, in addition to physical sensations, your own feelings should also be observed. First, find a posture that is comfortable and stable and allows you to keep your body still for about 20 min. Maintain a straight back  so that you can breathe freely. Breathe deeply into your stomach and out again. The breath is your anchor. And then slowly let your eyes fall shut. Now first perceive your body. How does it feel? If you feel any tension in your body, try to make it soft and relaxed. Also, let the muscles around your eyes become soft and relax your jaw muscles. Relax your shoulders, your arms, and your hands. Relax your chest and your abdominal muscles, let your stomach be completely loose and soft. Consider what mood you are in right now. Are you, for example, excited, sleepy, or calm? Simply acknowledge your mood without judging it. Now imagine something that went particularly well in your life. A particularly positive experience that was accompanied by pleasant emotions. What do you feel when you think about it? Try to consciously perceive this emotion again. Can you also feel it in your body? Maybe it gets warm around your chest or you notice that you start to smile. Pay close attention to the positive feelings that a beautiful memory triggers. Other emerging thoughts and sensations of your body you can perceive, accept, and name.

And now, slowly direct your attention back to your surroundings. Pay attention to the sounds and the space that surrounds you. Feel the air on your skin and the light that shimmers through your eyelids. And when you are ready, gently open your eyes and now fully return to the outside world.

---

**Reflection**

The learners' reflection can be stimulated by the following questions:

- Was it easy for you to revive positive memories in your thoughts?
- What emotions did you feel during the positive thoughts?
- Were you able to particularly perceive the positive thoughts in a part of the body?
- Were you able to concentrate well on the positive feelings?

---

## Planning for the Upcoming Practice Week

1. Perform one of the two exercises daily.
2. Write down three things you are grateful for every day. It's best to keep this list in the morning, before the day has really started.

**Minute of Silence**

| | Gratitude | Meditation exercise |
|---|---|---|
| Monday | | |
| 1. | | |
| 2. | | |
| 3. | | |
| Tuesday | | |
| 1. | | |
| 2. | | |
| 3. | | |
| Wednesday | | |
| 1. | | |
| 2. | | |
| 3. | | |
| Thursday | | |
| 1. | | |
| 2. | | |
| 3. | | |
| Friday | | |
| 1. | | |
| 2. | | |
| 3. | | |
| Saturday | | |
| 1. | | |
| 2. | | |
| 3. | | |
| Sunday | | |
| 1. | | |
| 2. | | |
| 3. | | |

# References

Merkl, H. (2022). *Erkenne dein wahres Selbst und lebe dein lichtvolles Potential!* Novum pro.

# 11

## Course Unit 8: Building Mindfulness

**Goals**

- Building mindfulness in everyday life
- Planning mindfulness exercises
- Forming habits

**Content: Living in the here and now**
A mindful lifestyle can only be achieved if exercises are regularly incorporated into everyday life. To create habits, various methods can be applied. One can attach the mindfulness exercise to an already existing habit, create reminders, plan how to deal with obstacles, or reward oneself after the work is done.

**Procedure**

- Minute of silence
- Recapitulation of the last exercise week
- Psychoeducation
- Exercise 1: Observing Breath with Labeling
- Reflection on Exercise 1
- Story "Temple of 1000 Mirrors"
- Exercise 2: Mindfulness Meditation
- Reflection on Exercise 2
- Exercise 3: Evaluation of Benefits and Creation of a Training Plan
- Minute of silence

**Exercise 1: Observing Breath with Labeling**

- Close eyes
- Participants focus on their breathing
- Emerging thoughts are named (labeled)

© The Author(s), under exclusive license to Springer-Verlag GmbH, DE, part of Springer Nature 2024
D. Jekauc et al., *Mindfulness Training in Sport*,
https://doi.org/10.1007/978-3-662-68804-5_11

## Exercise 2: Mindfulness Meditation

- Dwell in the here and now
- Being carried away by thoughts, but always returning to the here and now
- Attempt not to follow thoughts, but just to perceive them

## Exercise 3: Evaluation of Benefits and Creation of a Training Plan

- Planning how mindfulness training could be integrated into everyday life
- Creation of a training plan for the coming weeks

## Building Mindfulness

### A Minute of Silence

Each course unit begins with a minute of silence to arrive in the here and now.

### Implementing Mindfulness

In the last unit of the eight-week mindfulness program for athletes, the foundation should now be laid to independently carry out the techniques learned in the past weeks in the future. For this, everyone should find their own way. One should consider how it can be possible to plan one's own future with mindfulness and to make mindfulness a habit. But how could this work?

It helps, as the last eight weeks have probably shown, to regularly practice the exercises in a constant setting. For example, one can plan to consciously enjoy mindfulness for half an hour in the morning. Often it helps not to set a fixed time, but to tie in with existing habits. Do you drink coffee first thing every morning? Then you can plan to do a mindfulness exercise after this coffee. Do you check emails one last time at the end of a workday? Then you can always follow this with a small meditation.

To promote your planning, you can also use reminders. For this, for example, you hang a reminder on the bathroom mirror that you want to enjoy a moment of mindfulness after brushing your teeth. But one should not only think about opportunities to carry out the plans, but also plan obstacles. It is to be expected that, if you answer the phone once, you will have a hard time getting rid of the person on the other end of the line. Make a resolution: If the phone rings before an exercise, I won't answer! The formulation of these if-then sentences with opportunities (e.g., "If I have brushed my teeth, then I enjoy a moment of mindfulness") as well as hurdles

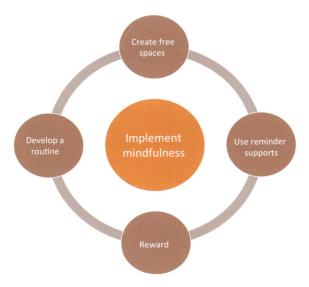

**Fig. 11.1** Implementing Mindfulness

(like the ringing of the phone) can help one in planning and implementing his exercise phases.

And if, despite all these measures (Fig. 11.1), you still have difficulties carrying out what you have planned, then you can try to reward yourself for successfully completing your exercise units. This not only associates the exercise with a positive feeling, but also increases the anticipation of being able to complete the exercise.

In the end, however, everyone has to find their own way. Some find it easier to implement habits, others have to resort to all tricks. Consider what role mindfulness should play in life, and implement this in your own way.

## Practical Exercises and Reflection

### Exercise 1: Observing Breath with Labeling

#### Background Information
Starting position: Upright, but comfortable seat
Duration: 20 min
Benefits: Training of concentration, which is a necessary resource for meditating and for subsequent mindfulness exercises, as well as the generation of a relaxation effect, training of conscious perception of thoughts

## Instructions for Implementation

To focus on your breath, find a sitting position where you can sit comfortably for an extended period. Calm your body by finding a comfortable and stable posture where you can breathe easily and naturally into your belly. If you like, close your eyes and focus your attention on the here and now. Feel what your body feels like. Are there specific sensations, tensions, or pains? Where is the body relaxed and at ease? Pay attention to the sounds around you and the feelings that move you internally. Fear or tension? Hope, affection? And what thoughts and expectations push themselves to the forefront? All of this belongs to you and your life: sensations, feelings, and thoughts. Now consciously realize that you are breathing alongside all these sensations. Use the movement of the breath to practice staying present with your attention. Observe your breath very closely, how do you perceive it? A coolness at the back of your throat when inhaling? The warmth of the exhaled air? A tingling? The movement of your chest? The belly rising and falling? Feel your breath, but try not to change or control it. Simply become aware of it and let it find its own rhythm. For the next ten minutes, simply feel your breath as it flows in and out. No matter where it makes itself noticeable: in the nose, throat, belly. You will notice that your thoughts wander. Plans or memories distract you. If, while following your breath, thoughts arise that capture you and you lose yourself in them—these can be images or words, memories or plans—then give these thoughts a name. Call them, for example, simply "planning" or "remembering". Normally these thoughts dissolve when you become aware of them. Your attention works similarly to sunlight on fog. The thoughts disappear and you can return to your breath. Sometimes, if it is a very intense, strong thought, it will not disappear immediately. Then simply continue to name it "remembering", "planning" or "thinking" until it disappears. And then return to your breath. Imagine how the breath brings oxygen into your body, which is absorbed into the blood in the lungs and distributed throughout your body with every beat of your heart.

When you are ready, slowly direct your attention back to your surroundings and prepare to open your eyes again.

### Reflection

The learners' reflection can be stimulated by the following questions:

- How did you perceive your breath? Where did you feel it?
- How well were you able to stay focused on your breath?

# 11 Course Unit 8: Building Mindfulness 121

- Did you have many thoughts going through your head? Or did your thoughts perhaps wander less often?
- If you drifted away from your breath, were you able to find a name for your thoughts and was one category particularly frequent?
- Were you able to return to your breath after you had drifted away?
- How did the exercise feel compared to the previous week?

## Story for Reflection: Temple of 1000 Mirrors

"In a distant land, a long time ago, there was a temple with a thousand mirrors, and one day a dog came along. The dog noticed that the gate to the temple of a thousand mirrors was open and cautiously and fearfully he opened the gate and went into the temple. After he had entered the temple, he believed he was surrounded by a thousand dogs. He began to growl, and he looked at the many mirrors and everywhere he saw a dog that was also growling. He became increasingly aggressive and he began to bare his teeth, and at the same moment, the thousand dogs began to bare their teeth, and the dog became frightened and ran out of the temple in panic as fast as he could. This terrible experience had deeply ingrained itself in the dog's memory and he believed that all other dogs were evil. The world was a threatening place for him, and he was shunned by other dogs and lived bitterly until the end of his days.

Time passed, and as luck would have it, another dog came along one day. The dog noticed that the gate to the temple of a thousand mirrors was open and curiously and expectantly he opened the gate and went into the temple and believed he was surrounded by a thousand dogs. And the dog began to smile, and he looked at the many mirrors and everywhere he saw a dog that was also smiling. And he began to wag his tail with joy and at the same moment, the thousand dogs began to wag their tails, and the dog became even happier. He had never experienced anything like this, and full of joy he stayed in the temple as long as he could, playing with the thousand dogs. This beautiful experience had deeply ingrained itself in the dog's memory. From then on, he saw it as proven that other dogs were friendly towards him. The world was a friendly place for him and he was well-liked by other dogs and lived happily until the end of his days." (quoted from Steuer, 2019, p. 29). *quote translated from German*

## Discussion

In addition to the interpretations of the learners, the following approaches can also be discussed (in the group):

- The growling dog is surrounded by growling dogs and the smiling dog by smiling ones. We construct our world: We see what is within us, not what the world is. Our own feelings influence our perception of the outside world, such as the perception of team colleagues or an opposing team.
- Actually, it's just a temple with mirrors, but for one dog it becomes hell and for the other a wonderful place. Each person perceives a situation differently.
- The perception of situations can be a mirror of one's own thinking and actions.

### Exercise 2: Mindfulness Meditation

**Background Information**
Starting position: Comfortable, but upright sitting position
Duration: 20 min
Goal: Building non-judgmental presence in the here and now

### Instructions for Implementation
In this meditation, we want to try to stay in the here and now, without judging any thoughts or feelings that arise. First, find a posture that is comfortable and stable, allowing you to keep your body still for about 20 min, with a straight back and so that you can breathe freely. And then, let your eyes slowly close. First, become aware of your body. How does it feel? Let the day pass by you once again. If you feel any tension in your body, try to let it soften and relax. Now let the muscles around your eyes soften and relax your jaw muscles. Also relax your shoulders, your arms, and your hands. Relax your chest and your abdominal muscles, let your stomach be completely loose and soft. Consider what mood you are in right now. Are you, for example, excited, sleepy, or calm? Simply acknowledge your mood without judging it. Now detach yourself from the sensations of your body and arising thoughts and feelings. Try to think of nothing. Push thoughts, feelings, and sensations aside and just be present. Whenever thoughts arise and carry you away, then detach yourself from them. Try not to follow them, but just acknowledge them. Always arrive back in the here and now.

And now slowly direct your attention back to your surroundings. Pay attention to the sounds and the space that surrounds you, feel the air on your skin and the light that shimmers through your eyelids. And when you are ready, gently open your eyes and now fully return to the outside world.

## Reflection

The reflection of the learners can be stimulated by the following questions:

- Were you able to arrive and stay in the here and now?
- Were you able to detach yourself from arising thoughts?

## Exercise 3: Evaluation of the Benefits and Creation of a Training Plan

**Background Information**
Duration: 15 min
Benefit: Implementation of mindfulness into everyday life

Each learner evaluates for themselves the benefit of the mindfulness training over the past eight weeks and creates a plan for the next weeks, when and how mindfulness training can be implemented into everyday life or training.

*Guiding questions for evaluating the benefits:*

- How much have I benefited from mindfulness training?
- What did I particularly enjoy?
- Which exercises have helped me to develop further?
- What do I want to implement in the future?

*Guiding questions for creating an individual training plan:*

- At what time has mindfulness training worked best for me?
- How can I make mindfulness a habit?
- What does my plan look like specifically for the next week?

**Minute of Silence**

# References

Steuer, D. (2019). *Die Weisheit des Universums: Weisheitsgeschichten zum Nachdenken*. BoD—Books on Demand.